The
UGLY
TRUTH
about
CASH

50 WAYS EMPLOYEES AND VENDORS CAN STEAL FROM YOU...
and What You Can Do About It

Ruth King

***BOOK*LOGIX**

Alpharetta, GA

State and local laws vary significantly and it is the responsibility of the user of this book to ensure that the activities suggested in this book comply with all laws that apply to the employer's, readers, and users of this book's operations.

The Ugly Truth about Cash: 50 Ways Employees and Vendors Steal from You is designed to educate and provide general information regarding the subject matter covered. However, state and local laws and practices vary from state to state and are subject to change. Because each reader and company is different and each situation in that company is different, specific advice should be tailored to that particular company and circumstances. For this reason, the reader is advised to consult with his or her own advisors regarding the individual specific situation.

The author has taken reasonable precautions in the research for and writing of this book and believes that the facts presented in the book are accurate as of the date written. However, neither the author nor the publisher assume any responsibility for any errors or omissions. The author and publisher specifically disclaim any liability resulting from the use or application of the information contained in this book, and the information is not intended to serve as legal advice or financial advice related to individual situations.

ISBN: 978-1-61005-935-0

Library of Congress Control Number: 2017919500

10 9 8 7 6 5 4 3 2   1 2 2 1 1 7

Printed in the United States of America

♾ This paper meets the requirements of ANSI/NISO Z39.48-1992 (Permanence of Paper)

DEDICATION

This book is dedicated to the millions of hardworking small business owners. May the stories in here help you protect your hard-earned cash.

To David,
Protect your
Cash!
Ruth King

CONTENTS

Contents

Part II: What You Can Do about It

FOREWORD

Jim Blasingame

At the end of a business day, you always lock the doors of your office, shop, and warehouse. And yet those properties probably have windows that can be easily breached.

You install a security system, but we all know that any determined intruder can do their worst and be gone before the authorities respond.

We've all heard the ancient proverb "Locks are to keep honest people out." So it would seem that locks are really for two purposes:

To inconvenience the bad guys—make them work a little harder to get at your stuff.

To tell the honest people that what's on the other side of the lock isn't free—you can't just wander in and help yourself.

After employees work for us for a while, we begin to trust them enough to toss them a set of keys to the building. Plus, we give certain employees access to financial controls. Obviously, with such gestures, we've deemed these people to be honest.

But are they more honest and resistant to temptation than the people we put locks on doors to deter? Of course, we hope so. But they're still people. Aren't they subject to all the character flaws, poor decision making, personal challenges, and shortcomings of any other human?

Ruth King thinks so. And she has the stories to prove it.

Ruth isn't a cynic. She's not down on humanity. But she is a world-class business management thought leader. To earn that credential, she's logged many hours with CEOs who didn't install the appropriate "locks" on access they'd given to once-honest employees who went rogue with the company assets.

There's another ancient proverb that goes "Trust in God, but tie your camel anyway." Ruth thinks you should apply this wisdom with even the most trusted employees, like those who have spent years with you in the trenches of the marketplace and have earned your trust.

In *The Ugly Trust about Cash*, Ruth identifies many different ways that trust was breached in various organizations, what can be learned from those instances, and how to avoid these problems. And if you find yourself feeling uncomfortable setting up checks and balances with your most trusted team members, think of it as beneficial for them: You're establishing standards and systems that essentially by definition exonerate them in the event of missing assets, because you shared oversight with them at every step. The result is you'll likely reduce breaches, and if one does happen, you'll be pretty sure who to rule out right away.

But there's much more to Ruth's book than someone you trust letting you down. She delivers the goods on how to improve your cash picture with better procedures, as well as how to find "found money."

Ruth has been a regular member of my Brain Trust on my radio program for many years. Of the thousands of people I've interviewed in 20 years, including hundreds of regulars, like Ruth, she's among an even smaller group of experts I consider to be the best of the best in their field. And Ruth's field is helping you have the maximum opportunity to be financially successful in your small business.

If you'll listen to Ruth, you'll significantly improve your chances of success. And the best way I know to do that is with this book, and any of her other books.

You'll use this book in two ways: First, you'll read it like you would any other book, front to back; then you'll keep it handy to use as a quick reference as you operate your business every day.

Take my advice and get close to Ruth King. You'll thank me later.

Jim Blasingame
Author of *The Age of the Customer* and *The 3rd Ingredient*
Host of *The Small Business Advocate Show*

WHY PEOPLE STEAL

In the 36 years I have been consulting with and coaching small business owners, one of the most difficult things I've ever had to do was tell two partners that a third partner was stealing at least $50,000 a year from their business. It probably was more. However, I felt horrible. I didn't want to dig any further (see story 6).

Theft is the most heart wrenching thing I have to deal with. You work hard. You never expect people to steal from you. When they do, your first reaction is disbelief, then sadness.

And nobody talks about it. Until now. It is time that someone did.

Small business owners like you work too hard and invest too many hours to have your money and other assets stolen. This theft could cause serious cash flow problems and damage your business if not caught. This book gives you simple, easy procedures to put in place to keep the honest people honest.

I believe that 99% of your employees are honest. Some people steal the first time because of need. Something has happened in their life (divorce, sickness, death), and they need money. They stop thinking rationally and get emotional. Then they do things they never would do when thinking rationally: stupid things like the bookkeeper in the first story that landed her in jail for three years because she forgot that the company loaned money to its employees. These are part of the 99% who are usually honest until tempted.

However, there are the remaining 1% of employees who get a thrill out of stealing, the professional embezzler. It is the challenge that's the draw. Can they get away with it? It is a joy to them. As one very wise man told me, "The job of a good embezzler is to become the trusted bookkeeper." The professional embezzler is very patient. She learns your processes or lack thereof. She works hard. She earns your trust.

Then, she takes a little. When you don't discover it, that little turns into tens of thousands of dollars, until she quits or gets caught. Most times she quits abruptly for no apparent reason. Then you find out about it later, when the next bookkeeper is hired.

It may not be your employees who are stealing from you. Your vendors can steal too. Their employees might be part of the 1%. Several stories in *The Ugly Truth about Cash* highlight how your vendors can change check amounts, create side deals with your employees, and more.

There are three major ways people steal: money, materials, and time. Most employees don't think twice about surfing the web, taking excessive smoking breaks or personal phone calls, or texting on company time. In fact, most small business owners accept and pay for a small amount of personal time as part of an employee's day. This book exposes how much that time theft really costs you.

All of the events in *The Ugly Truth about Cash* are real. I have guaranteed anonymity to the business owners who were willing to share their stories so that you can learn from what happened to their businesses and prevent it from happening in your business.

MY PERSONAL STORY WITH THEFT

My father was a brilliant trial defense attorney. One of the partners in his law firm handled all of the real estate closings for the firm. When the real estate market tanked and there were not many closings, people in the firm started wondering how he could maintain his lifestyle.

My father was focused on a different area of law and didn't pay much attention to the real estate transactions. One of the junior attorneys found out that other partner was stealing the closing fees and told my father. At first my father was like most business owners: he couldn't believe that this partner would do something like this. However, when he investigated it, my father found out that it was true.

He had this partner disbarred and making monthly restitution to him, the other partners, and subsequently their wives (including my mother) when the original partners passed away. The event also broke up his law firm.

I watched this unfold as a young adult. When my father passed away, I made sure that another attorney would handle the distributions. The attorney I chose? The one who found the theft and told my father.

This embezzlement had a great impact on me. I became very aware of business theft, how it hurts businesses, and the emotional impact on the business owners' lives.

I share these stories because I hope this never happens to you. Implement the suggestions in this book to keep the honest 99% of people honest, and use those tools to watch out for that remaining 1%.

PART ONE

STORIES

THEFT STORIES

These are stories of how employees and vendors steal from you and how you can protect yourself.

1.

MY BOOKKEEPER WAS GOING THROUGH A NASTY DIVORCE

Many years ago, when companies still got their bank statements and canceled checks in the mail each month, I needed a new bookkeeper. I found one who was competent. In the first three years she was with the company she produced accurate financial statements and made very few errors.

During her third year of employment her husband and she decided to split up. It was a nasty divorce and was affecting her work. We were understanding and told her to take as much time as she needed.

To make an already miserable situation more miserable, one day her attorney called her and said that if she didn't give him $3,000 within a week, he was dropping her case. She didn't have $3,000, so she forged a check, thinking, "I get the bank statements, and I will just pull the check out before I balance the checkbook. No one will ever see it."

A few days later, I got a call from my banker asking me if I knew Attorney X. I said no. The banker said that he had a check written to this attorney with a signature that looked odd so he decided to call.

I raced to the bank to look at the check. No, I didn't write and sign it. No, I don't know that attorney.

I went back to the office and confronted the bookkeeper. She denied it at first, then after more questioning, she broke down crying and admitted that she forged the check.

My comment to her: "Why didn't you just come to us? You know we loan money to our employees because you take the repayments out of their checks each week." She just looked at me.

Because she was thinking emotionally rather than rationally, she spent three years in jail for forging a check.

What I Learned:

- When normally honest people get in trouble, they stop thinking rationally and start thinking emotionally. This is where theft problems can begin if procedures are not in place to keep the honest people honest.

Implement these company procedures:

- Your bookkeeper should never have check signing authority (unless your bookkeeper is your spouse or owns a significant piece of the business). If the bookkeeper in this real-life story had had check signing authority, it would have been more difficult to prosecute her, because with check signing authority, you have given that bookkeeper the authority to write any check that she wants to write (see story 44). In this case, she didn't have check signing authority, so it was clearly theft and much easier to prosecute.

- Send your bank statements home. If the owner had received the statement at home, the bookkeeper knew that the owner would see the check first, and she would have been less likely to forge a check. Sending your bank statements home lets you see all of the check pictures before anyone else. You can make sure that the checks are correct and that your signature is on all checks, as well as be notified of bounced checks, late loan payments, and other banking issues.

2.

IN MY OPINION, THE SNEAKIEST AND MOST INGENIOUS WAY TO STEAL

I discovered this sneaky and ingenious way to steal from a company when a business owner called me and asked if I would help him make sure his pricing was correct. I said yes and asked him to send me his year-end profit and loss statements and balance sheets for the past two years.

When I got his financial statements, I put his expenses in my overhead calculation sheet to calculate his overhead cost per hour. The expense totals didn't match what was shown on his profit and loss statement. At first I didn't believe it, even though I was using Excel, and Excel never makes an addition mistake. So, I added up the numbers on an old-fashioned adding machine. The numbers didn't match.

I realized that this was the most creative way to steal I had seen in more than 30 years. No one, including me, thinks to put the numbers you see on your profit and loss statement into a spreadsheet to ensure the numbers match actual expenses. Until now.

Figure 1 shows the numbers from the company's profit and loss statement in comparison to the numbers I calculated.

You can see the differences.

There are some categories, like payroll expenses, where the spreadsheet matched the numbers on the business owner's profit and loss statement. However, there were many more categories that didn't add up.

When you total the numbers, my calculation was $51,765 less than what was stated on the company profit and loss statement.

Long story short: the owner's P&L said expenses were $637,510. The spreadsheet added to $585,745. There was more than $51,000 missing!

Figure 1

Overhead Cost Per Hour

Overhead Expenses	Excel	on P&L
Depreciation Expense	4,065	
Sales Tax	1,184	
State Sales Tax	7,721	
Local Sales Tax	15,371	
County Sales Tax	2,551	
Total Sales Tax	30,892	26,827
Freight	297	
Mitigation Expense	2,815	
Advertising	32,184	
Direct Mail	37,298	
Internet	30,771	
Print Advertising	9,414	
Promotional	24,074	
Referrals	200	
Telephone	3,404	
Total Advertising	140,458	137,346
Auto Expense	-1,003	
Auto DMV	6,211	
Auto Gas	42,983	
Auto Insurance	518	
Auto Repair and Maintenance	11,331	
Dustin's Truck Lease	5,772	
GPS	3,619	
Total Auto Expense	69,492	69,432
Fresno Rent Expense	500	
Shop Rent Expense	8,400	
Utilities	6,040	
Total Shop Rent Expense	14,940	14,440
Storage	584	
Uniforms	10,679	
Water	1,425	
Total Direct Operating Costs	255,781	234,405
Accounting	23,790	
Bad Debts/NSF Bounced Check	-17,953	
Bank Charges	329	
Bank Fee	55	

Credit Card Fees	54,197	
ITEX Fees	303	
Total Bank Charges	60,722	54,855
Business Licenses & Permits	6,879	
Charitable Contributions	2,409	
Continuing Education	14,816	
Dues & Subscriptions	6,052	
Employee Reimbursements	820	
Finance Fees	436	
Insurance	10,301	
Health Insurance	6,251	
Insurance - Liability	14,440	
Insurance Interest	354	
Total Insurance	62,560	31,346
Interest Expense	1,085	
Legal & Professional Fees	6,030	
Meals & Entertainment	14,599	
Office Expenses	12,941	
Other General and Admin Expenses	3,806	
Payroll Expenses - Office	0	
Employers Share PR Taxes - Office	7,785	
Salary and Wage - Office	88,462	
Total Payroll Expenses - Office	96,247	96,247
Shipping & delivery expense	1,294	
Software	20,284	
Quickbooks Payments Fees	3,542	
Total Software	25,120	23,826
Stationery & Printing	1,189	
Taxes & Licenses	3,204	
Telephone/Cell/Online Expenses	19,584	
Travel	10,016	
Travel Meals	879	
Utilities Home Office	4,265	
Total Administrative	283,109	322,246
Payroll Costs	0	
Salary and Wages	0	
Salary & wage - Installation	52	

Salary & wage - Service	958		
Salary & Wage - Office	250		
Total Salary and Wages	1,260	1,260	
Payroll Expenses	0		
Company Contributions	0		
Retirement	413		
Taxes	3,874		
Wages	38,436		
Total Payroll Expenses	42,722	42,722	
Refund Customer Satisfaction	2,712		
Travel	161		
Total Expenses	585,745	637,510	51,765

What I Learned:

- This is a great way to steal. You almost never add up the numbers on the P&L. You assume that they are right. $51,000 out the door is easy to hide because of your assumption. A few dollars here, a few dollars there—no one will ever catch it!

Implement this company procedure:

- Enter the expenses stated on your P&L into a spreadsheet. Make sure they match. You don't have to do it every month. Do it a few times a year.

3.

A TRUSTED EMPLOYEE WAS STEALING PETTY CASH

I kept petty cash in two places: less than $200 in a locked cash box and several thousand dollars in a safe that held the cash we didn't want to keep in the cash box. This money eventually was deposited in our operating account.

The bookkeeper was responsible for counting the petty cash and reporting it once a month on the financial statements. She delegated this responsibility to an employee who seemed to be honest and hardworking and rarely, if ever, missed a day of work. In addition, this employee was financially secure and didn't need to work.

The bookkeeper trusted this employee and stopped verifying the amount of petty cash that she reported on the balance sheet each month. One day the bookkeeper went into the safe to find some documents. She noticed that the petty cash that was there seemed to be a lot less than was reported. She counted it and found that $6,000 was missing. This was strange, and she came to me.

Only three people had access to the safe and the petty cash lock box. One person almost never dealt with petty cash, and the bookkeeper, who had access to the safe, had delegated the responsibility for it to the other person.

It had to be this third person. I brought all three employees into my office one at a time. I asked the same questions to all three, watching their reactions when I asked the questions (in addition to listening to their answers). The person who I assumed took the cash was totally uncomfortable with the questions and her story changed from day to day. Originally she said that the money was in the lock box and someone stole it from the box. I got $6,000 from the bank (which I immediately put back in) and asked her to put the $6,000 in the cash box. Obviously it didn't fit.

Deduction: she had to have stolen the money.

I was shocked. She was the last person I ever thought would steal. She didn't need the money. She had been with the company for many years, showed up on time, did her job accurately and on time, was willing to work overtime when necessary, and was, from my perspective, a good employee.

I fired her and instituted more stringent petty cash reporting procedures. I now count the petty cash occasionally, and never at the same time each month.

What I learned:

- Remember that the job of a good embezzler is to become the trusted bookkeeper.
- Someone who is not the person dealing with day-to-day petty cash must verify the cash amount reported on the financial statements every month and not assume that the person handling it can be trusted.

Implement these company procedures:

- Petty cash must be verified each month. If money is taken from petty cash, receipts must be given for that amount. When the petty cash gets low, the amount of the receipts is replaced with a check cashed at your bank.
- Don't keep thousands of dollars in petty cash. Put all amounts over a few hundred dollars in your bank.
- Even if you have two people handling petty cash, the owner should count it occasionally.

4.

I ALMOST HIRED AN EMBEZZLING CFO

My longtime CFO was moving to another state. She gave me plenty of notice and said she would train her replacement.

I appreciated her willingness to leave on good terms and help the new CFO navigate the nuances of how we handle our accounting.

I reached out to my friends and colleagues, asking them whether they knew of a competent CFO looking to make a career change. A friend suggested a woman and I contacted her.

She came in for the first interview. She passed. My current CFO and I liked her. We both thought she could do the job.

The next step was a comprehensive bookkeeping test. We give this test to any person who wants an accounting position at our company. This test weeds out the people who interview well and appear to know accounting, but don't really understand debits and credits.

She passed the bookkeeping test with flying colors.

The final step was a background check. This is where we were shocked. She had been convicted of embezzlement! This was public record. She didn't mention this conviction in any of the interviews. She knew that had she mentioned it, there would be no chance of being hired. She was betting that we wouldn't do a background check.

We didn't hire her. The colleague who recommended her didn't know of the conviction until I told him.

We did find a very qualified CFO who picked up the nuances of our business quickly. The current CFO trained him and was available for questions when she moved.

What I Learned:

- The interview process must include a background check. It is your hard-earned money that the bookkeeper will be handling. A clean background check gives you a little comfort.

Implement these company procedures:

- Administer a bookkeeping test. Email me (rking@ontheribbon.com) if you would like a free copy of the bookkeeping test and answers.
- Complete a background check. This should be done for all prospective employees, not just prospective bookkeepers. If you have employees who go to customers' homes or businesses, background checks are essential. Many companies can provide a good background check for a small investment.
- Drug test applicants before hiring. Many companies also drug screen prior to hiring. This is critical with businesses where employees drive company trucks or go to customers' homes or businesses.

5.

DON'T GIVE OUT BONUS CHECKS

One of our company perks is a bonus based on company profitability. This bonus is given every year in February, never at the Christmas holidays. We don't want employees to think that it is a "Christmas bonus" and should be expected, even in years where company profitability is not good.

This year the bonuses were large because the company was very profitable. It was fun to share the profits with the employees. We had a company meeting where we handed out the checks.

Unbeknownst to us, one of the employees was so thrilled with the amount of his check that he bragged to all of his friends about it. How did he brag? He took a picture of it and put it on Facebook!

And yes, the picture clearly showed the check amount and the bank routing and account numbers.

We got a call from our banker, who questioned some large withdrawals from our bank account to a unusual location. We immediately told him that we didn't authorize any withdrawals and the banker shut down our operating account. It was caught in time before too much damage was done.

Then we investigated and found out about the check on Facebook.

We told the employees what happened. We didn't say who did it. However, we explained the consequences of doing this, and they understood.

Next year, bonus checks will be direct deposited into their checking accounts so that this cannot happen again. Employees will receive a receipt showing the deposit, just as they get for their regular paychecks.

What I learned:

- Employees who are emotional do not think rationally. This employee wanted to prove to his friends that he got a great bonus. He wasn't thinking about the consequences when he snapped a picture of the check and put it on Facebook.

Implement these company procedures:

- Consider direct deposit for your payroll checks. When you use direct deposit, employees get a notice of their gross wages and deductions. They see that a certain amount was put in their checking account. Employees cannot see the company's checking account and bank routing numbers.
- If direct deposit is not an option, have a separate payroll account where you keep just enough money to fund payroll each payroll period. Then, if an employee puts a picture of his payroll check on Facebook, hackers can get little or no money.

6.

DON'T USE SIGNATURE STAMPS

I started a business with two other partners. I was focused on sales, one partner on operations, and the other partner did the books. It was the perfect startup because each manger was focused on a critical area of business.

We decided that two signatures were necessary for any check that was written on the company bank account. The thinking was that two signatures would make all owners aware of money going out of the company. This seemed to be a good practice too.

One of the owners started to have health problems and was not present in the business as much. We decided to have a signature stamp made of his signature and gave it to the partner who was responsible for the financial segment of the business.

This was the wrong person to give the signature stamp to. Why? This partner was embezzling at least $50,000 a year from the business!

How did he do it? Whenever he wrote a company check, he had two signatures: his and the signature stamp. He coded the check to whatever he felt would not be noticed. Fifty thousand dollars is less than $1,000 a week. Usually he coded it to things that would not be noticed because the expenses were very large as a rule.

I usually didn't pay attention to the financial statements. After all, I trusted my partners. I decided just to check a statement. What caught my eye was that the financial partner coded some checks to penalties. I knew that the company paid their payroll taxes on time so I started investigating when he was not there. I found the checks from the bank statements and knew what was going on. Going back at least a year, the theft added up to more than $50,000. Quite frankly it was probably more, but I was sick to my stomach and quit investigating there.

I told the nonembezzling partner and we confronted the thieving partner. We showed him the proof. We decided not to prosecute him because we were in a small town and couldn't stand the embarrassment. In fact, we didn't fire him either.

What I learned:

- Even with signature stamps a partner not directly involved with the finances must review the bank statements.
- All partners must review the financial statements each month.

Implement these company procedures:

- Do not use signature stamps. If you require two signatures on checks, they should be two signatures, not a signature and a signature stamp.
- Review financials every month. The other partners trusted the financial partner and never looked at the statements each month. Had they

done so, they might have seen the penalty expenses and questioned them.

7.

MY AUTO REPAIR SHOP TRIED TO STEAL FROM ME

One of the lessons Ruth King taught me was to send my bank statements home and look at them before giving them to the bookkeeper to balance the books.

I started doing what she suggested. One month I noticed a check to our auto repair shop that seemed higher than I remembered.

The next morning I brought the bank statement to the bookkeeper and asked her to pull up the information and image of the check for the auto repair shop that we used.

The invoice from the auto repair company showed about $49. I signed a check for the $49. The amount taken from our account on the bank statement was $449. The check picture on the bank statement showed $449.

Someone in the auto repair shop had altered the check and added $400 to the check!

I took the bank statement, the invoice for $49, and the check stub showing the check for $49 to the bank. They credited my account for the $400 and went after the auto repair shop for the funds.

What I learned:

- I never thought that a vendor would steal from me. I looked at the bank statements to make sure my employees were not stealing from me. As it turned out, dishonest vendors' bookkeepers can steal too.

Implement this company procedure:

- Always send your bank statements home. This is the first line of defense against the 1% who are professional embezzlers. Look at the copies of the checks. You signed the checks. If something doesn't look right, you can spot it and ask the bookkeeper for backup. Another great reason for sending your bank statements home is you see all of the bounced checks, late payments, etc. associated with your bank account. It's your hard-earned cash. Watch what is going on with it.

8.

MY PAYROLL CLERK WAS OVERPAYING HERSELF

The company had grown to the point where I needed someone to handle payroll on a part-time basis. The bookkeeper and I hired a woman who we thought could prepare the weekly payroll. We agreed on an hourly wage and approximately 20 hours per week.

After some training she was able to handle each week's payroll accurately. I sign all the payroll checks and watch the amounts of each week's payroll.

In certain times of the year, payroll is larger because of employee overtime. I expect this, and we have the cash flow to take care of the additional payroll. It is during these times that the part-time payroll clerk also works a few extra hours to prepare payroll, so I expect her payroll check to be higher too.

When the busy times were over, there was very little overtime. Payroll checks became smaller again. I noticed that it appeared that the payroll clerk's check wasn't going back to normal. I knew what her hourly rate was, and the check seemed to be larger than I thought it should be.

I let it go. I thought that if she had made a mistake, she would come to the bookkeeper or me and tell us. The correction could be made the following week.

On the second week's payroll, I didn't see the hourly amount that I expected to see. I called her into my office and asked her to print out a report with the hourly rates for all of the employees.

She went back to her desk to do it. I could log on to her computer from my office and watch what she was doing. Sure enough, she was changing her hourly rate back to what we had agreed upon when we hired her.

She came into my office with the report showing all of the wages, including her correct wage. I told her what I had done and that I saw her change her payroll rate. I fired her on the spot.

What I learned:

- If something doesn't look right, question it. I took action immediately. I gave her the benefit of the doubt and the ability to come to me saying she made a mistake the first week. When she didn't admit a mistake, and her payroll amount was wrong for the second time, I asked for the employee wages list.

Implement these company procedures:

- Watch what you sign. If a payroll check looks wrong, question it and ask for backup.
- If you can't log in to your employees' computers, walk to the person's desk and ask that person to print out the report you need while you are watching. This will also prevent changes before the report is printed and given to you.

9.

DON'T GET A DIVORCE IF YOUR WIFE IS THE BOOKKEEPER

My wife and I ran our business together. She handled the bookkeeping, and I managed sales and operations. It worked well for many years. Then we decided we couldn't live together and work together anymore.

The divorce was nasty and messy because our business and personal lives were intermingled.

Even though my wife handled the bookkeeping, she never was a signatory on the checking account. I was the only one who could sign checks.

My soon-to-be-ex-wife decided not to pay payroll taxes when she prepared the payroll checks. She never told me. This was her way of getting back at me.

I was busy running the business. When I signed the payroll checks I never thought to question whether the payroll taxes were being paid. Since they were always paid during our years of marriage, I assumed that they were still being paid.

Soon after the divorce was final, I received a notice from the Internal Revenue Service demanding payroll taxes, interest, and penalties for the previous four quarters' payroll. I was shocked.

When I investigated, I found that she had not paid the payroll taxes for a year. And, since she was not a signatory on the checking account, she was not responsible for paying them. The Internal Revenue Service could not demand payment from her.

My wife wanted to "get me" and she did. This was a very expensive lesson to learn.

What I learned:

- The only people responsible for payroll taxes are those people who are signatories on your operations checking account. Since my wife couldn't sign checks, she was not responsible for payroll taxes.

Implement these company procedures:

- Always make sure that payroll taxes are paid. If you file them electronically, the confirmation numbers should be printed out and put somewhere for safekeeping. If the IRS should send you a letter saying the taxes for a quarter were not paid, you can give them the confirmation number from when you paid the taxes.
- Always make sure that the entry is correct. Sometimes when paying the payroll taxes, the person entering the information enters the correct amount of tax but specifies the wrong quarter. If this happens, the confirmation number shows that the taxes were paid on time but the time period they apply to was wrong. Correct this immediately.

10.

THE BANKRUPTCY COURT MADE ME GIVE A PAYMENT BACK

Our company was installing heating and air-conditioning equipment for a new building. The general contractor, who was our client, was known in the area. For our company, it was a large, yearlong job to which we had allocated sufficient field labor and materials to complete each phase of the project on time.

Our company received payments monthly for work that was done the previous month. At the job start, payments were received on time and our company met the time deadlines for the completed phases. As the job progressed, the payments from the general contractor got later and later. However, the company was still paid eventually. We started working on the job only when checks were received and the project started falling behind the expected completion date. Our rule was no work unless a check was received for previous work.

Rumors were flying that the contractor was in trouble. However, we were persistent about collections and still got paid, later than the company was supposed to be paid, but the company was paid. So, our company continued working on the project.

One day I received a bankruptcy notice in the mail. The general contractor filed bankruptcy. Work on the project stopped. Our company was owed only a small amount of money for work done the previous month. The field labor had enough other work to do so that it didn't severely impact the company's cash flow and profitability.

Several months later, during the bankruptcy proceedings, I got a notice to repay the payments made to my company for work done on the project. The trustee was requesting a check for approximately $60,000, the value of the checks received for work that had been done in the 90 days before the contractor filed bankruptcy. This would be a significant impact on the company's cash flow. That wasn't right!

In conversations with my attorney and the bankruptcy trustee, I learned that the bankruptcy court has the right to request return of payments made to vendors for up to 90 days prior to the bankruptcy filing. The trustee didn't care about the impact this would have on my company's cash flow. He just cared that he received the check.

I set up payments with the trustee to pay all $60,000 into the bankruptcy court. And it made me mad every time I wrote a check.

Yes, I would get some of it back, months later. And no, I didn't get all of it back. My money got distributed to the attorney and other vendors owed by the contractor who went bankrupt.

What I learned:

- My policy is right. Our field labor works on jobs only when it has been paid for the previous month. However, I couldn't have predicted that the general contractor would go bankrupt and the trustee would request repayment to the court for the previous 90 days of work.

- The fact that my bookkeeper was persistent in collecting the funds owed to us actually backfired in the end. Our persistency made our company get paid before other companies working on the job. So, the funds were redistributed "fairly," according to the bankruptcy trustee.
- I now keep a cash reserve to ensure that this cash situation won't impact us in the future.

Implement these company procedures:

- Make sure that, whenever possible, the construction jobs are bonded, i.e., if the general contractor can't pay, the bonding company will pay. If this job had been bonded, when it ended up in bankruptcy court, the bonding company would have been responsible for payment.
- Check out the financial condition of a company prior to agreeing to work for that company. Even if a company is known, if that company goes bankrupt, your company may have to repay the bankruptcy court any monies received 90 days prior to the bankruptcy filing. Build and keep a cash reserve in this amount as your company is working on the job.
- Collections are critical to cash flow. If a payment has not been received in the time allotted for payment, the bookkeeper must make a call the next day to find out when a payment can be

expected. If you don't get a check, stop work. It's hard but necessary to do this.

11.

I WENT TO THE LADIES ROOM IN THE MIDDLE OF PREPARING A BANK DEPOSIT

I am a receptionist. I am also responsible for making all the bank deposit preparations for the company.

When the mail comes in, I open the mail and immediately stamp the checks with a "for deposit only" stamp that includes the bank account number. I then add that check's customer name and amount to the deposit slip.

Once the deposit is prepared, I give the deposit slip and checks to the bookkeeper or company owner to make the actual bank deposit.

One day after the mail had come, I was in the middle of preparing the bank deposit when I had to go to the ladies room.

I got up from my desk and went. I didn't put the checks in a drawer. I mistakenly just left them on my desk. Since nothing had ever happened and I would be back in a few minutes, I never dreamed that it would be a problem.

When I returned, the checks were gone. I was surprised and I immediately searched my desk drawer, thinking that I might have put them in the drawer. I asked the bookkeeper and other office personnel whether they had taken the checks. The answer was no.

They did tell me that they heard someone come in the door, but when they went to take care of that person, no one was there. The only thing that we could think of was that mystery person stole the checks.

Since the deposit was not complete, some of the checks had the stamp on them. Others did not. In addition, I could not remember everyone who we had received checks from.

It was embarrassing to have to call everyone I could remember that sent us a check, explain what happened, and ask them to put a stop payment on the check. Our company paid the stop payment fees.

Everyone I talked with was very understanding. We eventually got all of the checks replaced.

What I learned:

- I will never leave my desk again without locking up the checks. You never know who could be coming in the front door of the office.

Implement these company procedures:

- The person opening the mail should not be the person who makes the bank deposits.
- Whenever you are handling cash or checks and you leave your desk, lock the cash and checks up. It takes only a few seconds to steal them. You never know who will pass by your desk and take them.

12.

I WAS SIGNING CHECKS FOR ABC COMPANY (AND THE VENDOR IS ABC CORP.)

I sign all of the checks that are drawn on our company account. There are a lot of them, and I didn't pay attention to the exact name on the check I was signing.

In addition, I knew that sometimes the same vendor had names that didn't exactly match. For example, we might pay ABC and ABC Company. These two checks, even though they didn't have exactly the same name, went to the same company. That company always cashed them even if the name wasn't exact.

I put up with sloppy bookkeeping. Over the course of many years we had many bookkeepers. When a bookkeeper was in a hurry and didn't immediately find the vendor, she created another one for the same company. To her, it was quicker and got the check written that she needed.

It got confusing because some of the accounts payable were listed under one company name, and some were listed under the second company or even a third company name. However, I put up with it.

I started noticing that more checks were being written to two companies with similar names. When I questioned the bookkeeper about it, she blamed an assistant who put the payables in the wrong company name.

The mistake was corrected for a little while. Then I noticed it happening again.

This time I didn't say anything to the bookkeeper. Instead, I looked at the canceled checks in the bank statement. Sure enough, the backs of the checks were different. It was apparent that they were going to two different checking accounts. I checked previous months' statements. More of the same: two different checking accounts.

Now I was suspicious.

I called the real vendor and verified the accounts payable owed to that company. When I asked about the payables to the other similar-sounding name, they had no record of those amounts being due.

It hit me that someone was stealing from our company. I was shocked since the bills looked similar and the amounts being charged looked normal. If it wasn't the bookkeeper, she was in bed with the person behind ABC company (the company that looked similar to the real vendor's name).

I confronted the bookkeeper, who finally admitted the theft. She agreed to make restitution, so I didn't prosecute her. Obviously I fired her.

What I learned:

- I am now the only one who can make vendor additions to the accounting software.
- All of the duplicate vendor names have been cleaned up. Each vendor only has one vendor name.
- Watch what you sign carefully. If you think that something doesn't look right, don't sign the check and ask for the backup.

- Keeping your bookkeeper on her toes generally sends a message that you are checking.

Implement these company procedures:

- Owners or a company manager should be the only ones allowed to enter new vendors. The bookkeeper should be locked out of adding new vendors to your accounting software.
- Print out a vendor list once per quarter. Make sure there are no duplicate names. If you don't know how to do it, watch the bookkeeper as she does it.
- Always require backup for any checks you sign. This can include purchase orders, packing slips showing receipt of materials, and vendor invoices. Make sure they match!

13.

AN EMPLOYEE ACCEPTED A POSTDATED CHECK

It is our company policy to request payment for work performed at a customer's home when the service is performed. Our customer service reps make sure that the customers are aware of this policy. They ask the customer how she will be paying at the end of the service: cash, check, or credit card.

Mrs. Jones (not her real name) told the office that she would be paying by check. The office relayed this information to the employee visiting her home.

At the end of the repair, when the employee asked for payment (saying the office told him you would be paying by check), Mrs. Jones asked him if she could give him a check and date it for Friday (a few days later) since her husband got paid that day and the check would be good then.

Not knowing any better, the employee said yes. The customer gave him a check with Friday's date on it.

We waited until the following Monday to deposit the check. We thought that it would be enough time for the payroll check to clear.

The check bounced. We called the customer. No answer. We left messages and our calls were not returned. She ignored us and did not make any attempt to pay the amount owed.

Finally, we did our normal collection procedure: send a certified letter. If we do not get a response from the customer we take the customer to small claims court. When we went to court, she appeared for the court date. She told the judge that the company accepted the check written for Friday's date because that was the date her husband got paid.

The judge asked me whether this was true. I said yes. The judge said, "Case dismissed."

I asked him why. He said that the company knowingly accepted a check that did not have sufficient funds to cover the check.

What I learned:

- Never accept a postdated check. If it is returned marked insufficient funds, in most states you will never win the case in small claims court.

Implement these company procedures:

- Train your employees not to accept a postdated check. The checks should be written and dated the day the work was performed.
- Train your employees to look at the date on the check. Make sure it matches the date the work was performed.

Author's note:

I have seen many situations similar to this one where the company accepted a postdated check that turned out to be not good. Every company I know of in this situation lost in court. Some lost thousands of dollars.

14.

I PAID $3,718 FOR EMPLOYEES TO EAT AT THEIR DESKS

Our employee handbook states that employees get a 60-minute lunch break. This is an unpaid lunch break.

Most employees go out to lunch and return in an hour's time. They get back to work upon returning.

I noticed that at least once or twice a week a few employees took their lunch break and came back with lunch. They ate their lunch at their desks after their lunch hour.

The reason was always "I had to run errands during lunch so I stopped at a fast food drive-through to pick up lunch."

Other employees brought their lunch, ate at their desks, and then left an hour early. They took their lunch breaks at the end of the day.

The excuses for eating lunch at employees' desks was starting to drive me crazy. I decided to calculate how much an employee who eats lunch at her desk was actually costing me.

I watched this habit. Eating at the employee's desk took an extra 30 minutes of nonworking time. Since there was at least one person who ate at their desk every day, I used 30 minutes a day for a week. That was 2.5 hours per week. That equated to 130 hours a year I was paying for employees to eat lunch at their desks.

This was expensive. The hourly wage for the office personnel averaged $22 per hour. When I added the social security taxes and other benefits, eating lunch at their desks was costing me $28.60 per hour.

Each year I was paying $3,718 for the employees to eat lunch at their desks!

This was too much. I started enforcing the lunch rule and didn't allow eating at their desks anymore. I also insisted on using personal time off if someone wanted to leave an hour early rather than using their lunch hour.

What I learned:

- I never realized how much eating at their desks actually cost me. When I calculated the number, I stopped allowing eating at their desks and enforced the lunch hour policy. The employees weren't happy about it but complied.

Implement these company procedures:

- Lunch breaks are for lunch. Employees should not be eating at the office after they take their hour lunch break. This policy should be clear in your employee handbook.
- Check with the labor laws of your state. Some states require breaks and lunch periods that must be taken by employees. Follow your state regulations.

15.

AN EMPLOYEE STOLE A CHECK FROM THE BOTTOM OF THE BOX OF CHECKS

The bookkeeper kept the company's box of checks under her desk. Since her door was locked whenever she left for the day, no one thought anything about the box of checks being left unlocked in her office.

When she processed accounts payable and wrote checks, everything seemed normal. There wasn't anything unusual with the check numbers. They were in the correct numerical sequence since the check numbers for the accounts payable payments matched the check numbers on the checks.

One month, when she was balancing the bank statement, she noticed a check out of order. This check had a number that was much larger than the normal sequence of checks.

She got a copy of the check. Sure enough, it had my signature on it. This was puzzling to her, so she came to me and asked about the check.

I knew nothing about it. Yes, it looked like my signature. No, I didn't remember signing that check for that amount.

We went to the bank. The banker said that unfortunately since it had my signature on the check, the check was valid for payment. It was cashed for several thousand dollars.

Upon further investigation, I discovered that a company employee stole a check, scanned his payroll check, and cleaned up and used my signature to write a check payable to him on the stolen check.

What I learned:

- Checks should always be kept in a locked filing cabinet or drawer whenever they are not in use.
- I now pay payroll through direct deposit, and unless a vendor steals my signature, my employees can't do that anymore.

Implement these company procedures:

- All checks, whether from customers or blank company checks, should be kept under lock and key. Customer checks should be immediately stamped with "for deposit only" and the account number, and the deposit should be made quickly.
- Send your bank statements home. You as the owner would have caught the check out of sequence before the bookkeeper came to you with the issue.

16.

MY BOOKKEEPER WAS MAKING FAKE DEPOSITS IN QUICKBOOKS

The bank checkbook balance has never been the same as the QuickBooks check balance, so I didn't pay too much attention to the cash balance on our financial statements compared to the QuickBooks cash balance. If the bookkeeper told me that she balanced the checkbook, I believed her.

The bookkeeper was also responsible for paying our payroll tax payments. She kept copies of the payments in a book. One day I received a certified letter from the Internal Revenue Service stating that a specific quarter's payroll tax payments were not received.

I went to the book and it looked like the payment was made. It was paid in the wrong quarter. However, this got me wondering what else was not being done correctly.

She was sick one day and I went through her desk. There was a check the company had received from the government dated seven months prior that had never been deposited. Now, more suspicion.

I decided to balance the checking account myself. When I started digging, the customer payments were being recorded so when the customer paid, their account was cleared. It showed that they didn't owe any money to the company.

However, bank deposits didn't match the QuickBooks bank deposits. They were much lower. I went back 14 months until I found a month where the bank deposits matched the QuickBooks deposits.

Money was mysteriously disappearing from the QuickBooks undeposited funds segment of the balance sheet.

Someone in the company tipped her off that I was going through her desk. She disappeared and never came back.

I felt totally disheartened and sickened as I was going through the 14 months of bank statements. I decided to prosecute her, and I gave all of the information and proof that she had stolen from the company to the police department. That is where it is now.

What I learned:

- Always ask to see the statement of proof that the bank statement matches the QuickBooks balance. There is a report you can print out of QuickBooks to show that the statement balances with the bank statement.
- Never completely trust your bookkeeper. Verify what she is telling you.

Implement these company procedures:

- Part of the financial statement information you receive at the end of each month should include the balance report that your accounting software cash balance matches the bank cash balance.

- Verify that payroll tax and income tax payments have been made in the proper quarter. If not, rectify the mistake immediately.

17.

THE PAYROLL COMPANY DIDN'T PAY OUR PAYROLL TAXES

I like to support our local small businesses. If a small business uses our company's products and services, I like to reciprocate.

The owner of a local payroll company came to my office and asked for my business. He gave me reasons why an outside firm doing the company's payroll would be beneficial to me. I said yes.

This company started doing our payroll. We were happy with his service and everything seemed fine. We paid payroll and payroll taxes to his company. His company did all of the required reporting and payments to the federal, state, and local governments.

About three years after this firm started doing our payroll, I got a notice from the Internal Revenue Service that our payroll taxes had not been paid. The IRS said they hadn't received payments for six quarters.

There was no way this was correct. I researched and found the payroll and payroll tax payments that we made to the payroll company. We sent this information to the IRS as proof that we had paid them to the payroll company and that they were mistaken in sending us the notice.

The IRS came back and said that they didn't have any record showing that the payroll company had paid our payroll taxes. I called the payroll company and didn't get a response.

As it turned out, the owner of this local payroll company took our payroll taxes and those of many other small businesses in the area and fled. He stole hundreds of thousands of dollars. The Internal Revenue Service is still looking for him.

The IRS wasn't through with us. Even though we could prove that we paid the payroll taxes to the payroll company, the IRS never received them. We were still responsible since they weren't paid to the Internal Revenue Service. They were still due. The only thing that the IRS waved was the penalty. We had to pay the payroll taxes and the interest. We ended up paying the taxes twice.

What I learned:

- Always verify that payroll taxes have been paid, whether you have an internal employee or an external payroll company paying the taxes.
- Use a large, publicly held payroll company. Although this is not supporting local businesses, these companies are large enough that if the payroll tax payments that you paid to the payroll company are not made, it is their mistake and they are not likely to abscond with the funds.

Implement these company procedures:

- Using an outside firm to process your payroll can save time. Interview many and determine which one gives you the most value for your money spent.

- Always check to see that the payroll tax deposits have been made. The payroll company should give you the reports that they have been made. Check these with the Internal Revenue Service and your state and local departments of revenue.

18.

MY BOOKKEEPER WAS GIVING ME FINANCIAL STATEMENTS WITH NEGATIVE GROSS MARGINS

I didn't pay too much attention to the financial statements my bookkeeper prepared. I decided to find out what they really meant. I started noticing that the gross margins on the profit and loss statements varied a lot, and sometimes they were negative.

I knew that the gross margins couldn't be negative. That meant the company bought materials for $10 and sold them for $5. There was no way that our prices were lower than our costs.

When I asked the bookkeeper about it, she said that was the way the numbers came out and insisted that they were right.

In addition, the equation

$$\text{beginning inventory} + \text{purchases} - \text{ending inventory} + \text{cost of goods sold}$$

didn't balance.

There was definitely something wrong!

Here's what I found: the bookkeeper didn't make sure that the revenues for a month matched the expenses incurred to generate those revenues for the month.

I insisted on accuracy with respect to revenues and expenses. Now I could feel comfortable that the revenues and expenses matched each month. The gross margins started becoming more consistent each month. Yet, they still varied more than they should.

I checked our pricing. It was right based on the amount of materials and labor required to produce our products and services. There had to be an issue somewhere.

When I started digging even further I found that our material costs were out of line. This is what was causing the gross margins to fluctuate.

Materials were going out of the warehouse without being accounted for. There was a hole in the process, and no one was responsible for inventory and materials purchased and used.

I locked down the warehouse and instituted an ordering and inventory procedure. We counted inventory and did the same count every month for seven months. It was really painful and took a long time, especially that first inventory count.

The equation started balancing and was in balance by the end of the year. When I looked at everything, the company lost $250,000 in inventory that year: an extra $250,000 in wasted cash.

As I told all of my employees, I would rather have paid them that amount in bonuses. Instead material purchases evaporated.

What I learned:

- Understand what your financial statements are telling you. There is no way of knowing how much cash was wasted in previous years before I started paying attention.
- Have a materials and inventory procedure. Make one person responsible for inventory. If materials are missing, you have one person to go to.

Implement these company procedures:

- Make sure your bookkeeper matches revenues and expenses incurred to generate those revenues each month. If your gross margins are not consistent on a monthly basis, find out why.
- Have an inventory policy in place. There should be a procedure for ordering materials, getting materials to the jobsite or production line, and returning materials.
- Inventory should be counted at least once per year. If you find problems, it should be counted more often—monthly, if required—until the problems are resolved.

19.

MY EMPLOYEE MADE THE BANK DEPOSITS

I operate a retail flower shop.

I don't do my own books. I have an outside bookkeeping firm that does the monthly financial statements. Many of our customers pay us in cash. I spend my time creating beautiful arrangements that delight our customers.

Our business is thriving. Many times the bank deposits have hundreds of dollars in cash. I never went to the bank to make these deposits. I trusted one of my employees to make the daily bank deposit and concentrated on the flowers.

Once in a while I would get a bank notice that there was an error in the deposit. It was $10 or $20, never large amounts. I assumed that we just added the cash wrong.

It didn't happen every week. Looking back, it was happening about once per month, and I am now sure that I didn't get to see all of the bank notices. This employee got to the mail before I did and took the notices out of the mail.

I found out about it because it dawned on me that we should not have this many bank deposit errors. I knew that I counted the cash correctly. Sure enough, one day I got another notice that the deposit was short $10. The only way this could happen was if someone took that $10, and that someone had to be employee making the deposit.

I let it happen one more time and fired her. I never confronted her about the theft. It was easier just to let her go.

What I learned:

- Take the time to make your own bank deposits. When I started doing this, I found that it didn't take much time to do. I actually enjoyed that short break.

Implement these company procedures:

- Always send your bank statements home. You will receive notices of errors in deposits and other banking issues with your money. Had this owner done this, she would have seen all of these notices and could have investigated sooner.
- The person opening the mail should not make the bank deposits. This may not be practical for smaller companies, but it is preferable that owners make bank deposits whenever possible.

20.

MY BOOKKEEPER WOULD NOT TAKE A VACATION

I had what I thought was an extremely loyal employee. She did the books for our company and had for a long time. She came in early and stayed late to ensure that I got my financial statements on time every month.

I had the perfect employee: hardworking, dedicated, and accurate.

It dawned on me that she would never take a vacation. Yes, a day here or there, but never a full week. Her reason was that payroll was due every week and no one else could do payroll. This was true, so I didn't question it.

I didn't think about it much either because I didn't take vacations. Like the bookkeeper, a day here or there, but rarely a full week. My thinking was I didn't want to come back to a mess and have to clean up.

One day the bookkeeper got sick. She didn't come in. This was rare. We survived the day without her.

Then she was still sick for a second and third day. By this time I needed to get checks sent to vendors and payroll was due.

Someone had to do it, so I went into her office to do it myself.

Since I had an extra set of keys to her desk and the passwords to her computer, I could get into the accounting software and figure out how to do what needed to be done.

I went into her office and stumbled around in the accounting software. I found there were many payments made to vendors with direct payments (no check needed). I saw loan payments, credit cards payments, office supply company payments, gas card payments, and others I recognized. Then, there was one that I never saw before, a vendor that I didn't recognize.

I found consistent payments to this vendor for years! When I added it up, it was over $90,000. So, who was this vendor? There was nothing huge so I never would have noticed it unless I did what I had done: go into her computer accounting software.

It turned out she had been embezzling for years.

A little every month, not noticeable to me since I didn't sign a check, added up to a lot over the years.

What I learned:

- Make sure you see all payments, even those to companies with direct payments.
- There was only a little bit taken each month, so I didn't notice it. However, a little adds up to a lot over the years. My hardworking employee turned out to be a thief!

Implement these company procedures:

- See all of the cash withdrawals from your checking account. It is best to look at your bank balances online every day. You can see everything that is added and withdrawn from your accounts.

- Insist that everyone take at least a week's vacation. This way someone else has to do that person's job. This is when you find discrepancies.

21.

CASH WAS ALWAYS TIGHT

We had an employee who was responsible for accounts receivable. Her job included calling customers when receivables were not paid on time.

Every month we printed out an aged receivables list and kept track of who owed the company money and how much of it was current and past due.

Unfortunately we didn't always prepare the monthly financial statements in a timely manner. Many times I was looking at them three months later (January's financial statements were ready in April), so I didn't have a good grasp on the accounts receivable balance on the statement because it was from a few months ago.

However, I did watch the accounts receivable balances and was told when large checks were received. Despite the checks coming in, we were always tight on cash. Sometimes we just scraped by to make payroll. Other times we couldn't pay all of our vendors on time. This didn't make sense to me, given the amount of cash that was coming in the door.

I couldn't figure out what was wrong.

I asked to see an aged receivables list. It looked right. Then I compared the accounts receivable on the aged receivables list to the receivables stated on the balance sheet. That was right too. Something just didn't add up.

I had to dig further. When I looked at the journal entries for the months, I noticed cash withdrawals and entries to make accounts receivable on the balance sheet match the aged receivables report.

Since journal entries never appear on the financial statement, I never saw the changes. I only looked to see that the aged receivables report match the total receivables on the balance sheet and the aged payables report matched the accounts payable on the balance sheet.

When we dug deeper, we found that the accounts receivable clerk stole more than $100,000 over the time period she was there. She agreed to make restitution, so I didn't prosecute her.

What I learned:

- It's not enough to make sure that the receivables and payable reports match the amounts shown on the balance sheet. You need to look at the month-end journal entries too.
- If you think something is wrong, it probably is. I knew that cash was tight. That didn't make sense to me because I knew what checks were coming in the door.
- Getting financial statements three months late added to the problem. I didn't have an accurate memory of cash from a few months ago.

Implement these company procedures:

- Get your financial statements on time. It's hard to remember what happened 90 days ago. January's statements should be prepared by February 10 or at the latest February 15.

- Always match aged accounts receivable and accounts payable report balances to the amounts stated on your balance sheet. They should match.
- Ask for month-end journal entries when you receive your financial statements. Make sure that they make sense.

22.

AN EMPLOYEE HACKED OUR PURCHASE ORDER SYSTEM

We have a purchase order policy. Everything that is bought, from materials to office supplies to outside services, must have a purchase order. These purchase orders are computer generated.

The purchase orders must match the invoices that we receive from vendors (and in the case of materials, packing slips showing the materials were received) before the checks to the vendors are signed by me.

I thought the purchase orders system was tight and that nothing could be paid for before it was received. I was wrong.

It turned out that one of the field employees was using our accounts to purchase materials for his own company. The purchase orders were legitimate. The packing slips were legitimate. The payments to the vendor were legitimate. However, the materials were never used on our company jobs.

How did I discover this?

We get our financial statements every month. Our bookkeeper is meticulous about ensuring the numbers are right, so I am confident that the information I get each month is correct.

I noticed that gross margin was decreasing because our cost of materials was increasing. That didn't seem right, because we hadn't gotten notices from our vendors about price increases, and we hadn't given discounts to any customers.

I asked my bookkeeper to investigate. She assured me that the costs were correct and that everything we paid for had a purchase order and packing slips showing the materials were received.

The cost of materials was high again on the next month's financial statement. Something was definitely wrong.

I then pulled all the payments made to one of our vendors. I closely examined what was bought. I also knew what we had produced that month. The material purchases for that vendor seemed high for the month.

I went into the warehouse to see whether we had extra inventory from that vendor. The answer was no.

I looked at who ordered the materials (the purchaser's name is on the purchase orders). It was the usual group of people who bought materials. However, one thing stuck out. One of the employees seemed to be purchasing a lot more materials than normal. And, as it turned out, he went to the vendor to pick up those materials. They were not delivered to the company.

This employee was working for another company and used our company accounts to pay for their materials. This increased our costs, and they had no material cost to produce their products.

I fired him immediately and demanded payment for the materials that were purchased on our accounts. I'm not sure I got every dollar back, but I know I got most of the money returned.

What I learned:

- No system is foolproof. If someone wants to steal, they will find a way around the system.
- Had I not gotten accurate financial statements each month, I never would have caught the theft. I knew the numbers were right, so the decrease in gross margin signaled something was wrong.

Implement these company procedures:

- A good purchase order system is necessary. Make sure that purchase orders are filled out completely, including the materials purchased, the person making the order, and the price of the materials. Without knowing who ordered the equipment, the owner might not have found the culprit.
- Accurate, timely financial statements are necessary. If something doesn't look right, ask for backup and investigate the numbers.

23.

MY BOOKKEEPER HAD TOO MANY EXCUSES

My bookkeeper always made mistakes on the financial statements, and they were never on time. The mistakes were supposedly fixed but I never checked. After all, I barely looked at the financial statements. I was most concerned that we had the cash to pay payroll and our bills.

Then we decided to get a new computer system, which included new accounting software. Implementation was a nightmare. There were now more excuses. There was a glitch in the software. "The system won't let me tie payroll to job cost." "I can't make the accounts receivable balance the receivables report." Since I wasn't an accountant and I didn't understand the new accounting software, I took the bookkeeper at his word.

Financial statements came later and later.

Then a cash crunch hit. I didn't have enough cash to pay that week's payroll. Something was definitely wrong.

I called my CPA firm and asked for help. When the accountant came in, she saw that the system was so screwed up it was hard for her to follow any entries easily. Check receipts, bills sent to customers, or even where job costing and payments to vendors were not consistently entered. It was a mess. It took her a long time (and a lot of my cash) to straighten everything out.

The major thing that she did find was cash evaporating from the business checking account. It was apparent that the bookkeeper was embezzling funds from the company.

All the excuses and the mess he made were intended to hide the fact that he was embezzling.

With the accounting firm's help, I hired a competent bookkeeper. Now I don't put up with mistakes or excuses about late financial statements.

What I learned:

- Never accept excuses from your bookkeeper. If he's constantly offering excuses, either he doesn't know what he is doing or he is embezzling.
- Get someone you trust to oversee the bookkeeping. My CPA firm now comes in every six months to do an overview audit of the books. This gives me peace of mind that my financial statements are accurate.

Implement these company procedures:

- Good bookkeepers are mortified if they make a mistake. They pride themselves on preparing timely, accurate financial statements for your review. Look at the statements. If something doesn't look right, ask for backup. This sends a message to the bookkeeper that you are watching.

- The CPA firm who prepares your taxes should do a yearly review. They can also spot things that don't balance or look right. An outside firm looking at the numbers gives you peace of mind.
- Most bookkeepers have desks that are extremely neat. They know where everything is. This bookkeeper had a messy desk. He never knew where any backup paper work was and had to dig for it when asked. My guess is that he knew exactly where everything was and what he was doing. He just wanted to give the appearance of messiness.

24.

MY BOOKKEEPER WAS STEALING THE CASH RECEIVED FROM CUSTOMERS

Our company has service technicians who go to people's homes to repair their plumbing and HVAC systems. Technicians get paid when the repair is completed. A significant portion of our customers pay our technicians in cash. Of course we do get checks and credit card payments too.

Service technicians give their service tickets to the dispatcher along with the checks, cash, and approval codes for the credit card payments. The dispatcher puts her initials on the service tickets to signify that the money for the job was received. She then turns everything into the bookkeeper.

I never paid too much attention to the cash that came in the door. The bookkeeper told us stories of vacations she took, activities she did, and other outside interests. Given the expense of these activities I wondered how she could do all of them on her salary (she wasn't married and I didn't know of a trust fund or inheritance that she had received).

I let it go until a story about the latest vacation, which had to be very expensive. Then I got suspicious. There had to be a way that she was getting additional money to support these expensive habits. So, I started looking around.

It dawned on me that there was a lot of cash coming into the company. Whenever I made bank deposits there was always cash and checks. I wondered whether

I deposited all of the cash that customers had given us for work performed.

I went back through a month's service tickets. I added all of the cash that was given to the company. Then I looked through the bank deposits. The amount of cash received was not the amount of cash deposited.

I thought, *OK, maybe there was a mistake that month.* I looked at another month's service tickets and cash receipts. Again, the amount of cash received was not the amount of cash deposited.

After reviewing six months of service tickets and cash receipts, there was never a match between the money received and the bank deposit.

I started watching when the service technicians came in. Yes, they gave their service tickets and payments to the dispatcher. Yes, the dispatcher put her initials on the paperwork stating that she received the payments. Yes, she gave the tickets, cash, checks, and credit card receipts to the bookkeeper.

It had to be the bookkeeper. I couldn't believe it was her, yet I had to believe it was her. It was very disheartening because I trusted her. Unfortunately I now knew how she could afford those expensive vacations and habits.

What I learned:

- Always watch cash receipts. If there is a large amount of cash coming in, make sure that all cash gets deposited into the bank.
- If it sounds like a vacation or hobby is too expensive for an employee based on what you

are paying that employee, keep your guard up. There has to be a way they are funding that expensive vacation. You don't want to be paying for it on top of that person's salary.

Implement these company procedures:

- Always track cash coming in to the business. Make sure that all cash received is deposited in your operations checking account.
- The sign-off procedure was correct. It needed to go one step further to ensure that no cash was taken.
- If your employees regularly receive cash payments, there should be a maximum amount they are allowed to have without coming to the office to turn in cash.
- For retail operations, determine the maximum amount of cash that you will keep in the cash registers. Pull amounts over that limit and put them in the safe until a bank deposit can be made.

25.

OUR 401(K) PAYMENTS WERE LATE

Our company has a 401(k) retirement plan in place. Every payroll period we deduct the funds authorized by employees from their paychecks. We write a check for the total and send it to the company that administers our 401(k) plan for us.

I am friends with the broker who set up our plan. He comes every year and updates the employees and their accounts. I also see him socially.

One day I got a call from him, thinking that he wanted to set up a time to play golf. This was not a social call. He said that the company had not received checks for the retirement account for three months. He was concerned and wanted to know whether we had cash flow problems.

I was shocked. We didn't have cash flow problems and could have easily paid the amounts to the company. And I knew that not paying those payments could get me in trouble.

I asked him how much was due and wrote a check immediately. I asked whether he wanted to pick it up or have me send it. He said just to send the check.

Then I went to the bookkeeper and demanded to know why the payments weren't being made. She had a lame excuse.

I started digging. The payment for retirement deductions was not the only payment past due. Sales tax wasn't paid and the payroll taxes were late too.

We had the money to pay these payments. They just weren't paid. It was my fault for not paying attention and just trusting the bookkeeper. She is gone.

What I learned:

- Although this was not embezzlement per se, it cost us a lot of money in late fees, interest, and penalties. This was theft through incompetence. I blame myself for not paying attention to make sure that these payments are made each payroll period and on the days of the month they are due.

Implement this company procedure:

- Always know when payroll taxes, sales tax, and other payments are due. Put them on your calendar. Check on the due date to ensure the payments have been prepared or paid. Many of them are now done through direct withdrawals. In these cases, make sure you see the confirmation numbers proving the payments have been made.

26.

ONE OF MY TEAMS ALWAYS COMPLAINED ABOUT THE TIME ESTIMATED FOR A PROJECT

Project costing was never very important to me. As long as the gross margins were within the estimated range, I didn't pay attention to the projects. I just wanted to know that the customers were happy and they paid their bills.

One of our teams was always late finishing projects. They always complained that there was never enough time to finish a project in the time allocated for that project. They were usually late, and this has caused problems with customers from time to time.

Even though they complained about not having enough time, their projects came in at the required gross margin.

It never occurred to me to make sure their projects were profitable. If the gross margins were right, the projects should be profitable.

We hired a consultant who insisted on looking at all of the projects and the costs associated with each project. Her analysis is shown in Figure 2.

Customer	Sell Price	GP	GM	OH/hr	# Hours	Net Profit	Net Profit/hr
JE	$12,903.00	$5,227.01	40.51%	60.20	39.00	2879.21	$73.34
RP	$11,293.00	$4,918.10	43.55%	60.20	53.50	1697.40	$31.11
MC	$13,248.00	$5,119.03	38.64%	60.20	48.50	2199.33	$45.33
CF	$15,078.00	$7,074.60	46.92%	60.20	38.00	4787.00	$125.09
EK	$9,686.00	$4,495.27	46.41%	60.20	49.50	1515.37	$30.42
IR	$23,752.00	$11,809.49	49.72%	60.20	81.50	6903.19	$84.67
GP	$3,948.00	$2,488.82	63.04%	60.20	25.00	983.82	$39.96
HT	$5,644.00	$2,272.84	40.27%	60.20	59.00	-1278.96	-$21.37
DT	$11,020.00	$4,971.12	45.11%	60.20	72.00	636.72	$8.11
RR	$12,082.00	$6,498.91	53.79%	60.20	54.00	3248.11	$60.20
KP	$10,363.00	$4,990.82	48.16%	60.20	32.75	3019.27	$92.85
HG	$16,620.00	$6,852.43	41.23%	60.20	103.00	651.83	$6.03
DP	$30,352.00	$11,712.84	38.59%	60.20	150.00	2682.84	$17.50
DG	$2,519.00	$1,624.76	64.50%	60.20	14.75	736.81	$49.49
DG	$8,534.00	$4,336.98	50.82%	60.20	54.00	1086.18	$20.13
LP	$8,822.00	$1,712.35	19.41%	60.20	15.25	794.30	$52.00
ML	$7,489.00	$3,808.91	50.86%	60.20	39.00	1461.11	$37.91
RT	$8,545.00	$4,390.42	51.38%	60.20	30.25	2569.37	$84.58
RS	$10,931.00	$3,559.13	32.56%	60.20	90.00	-1858.87	-$20.11
TJ	$9,868.00	$3,910.69	39.63%	60.20	60.00	298.69	$4.68

Figure 2

It turned out that even with the same gross margin, I had one project that earned $73 per hour (customer JE) and another one where we paid our customer $20 per hour on the project (customer HT).

I also realized that this team, which continually complained about never having enough time, had the least profitable projects. We lost money on most of them. It turned out they were billing time to that project and not working on that project. They were stealing time.

That team was let go. We found and trained a new team.

What I learned:

- Pay attention to gross margin and the net profit on the projects. The net profit is more important than the gross margin.
- If a team is not profitable, find out why. They may be incapable of doing the work. or they may be stealing time.

Implement these company procedures:

- Determine the cost for doing every project your company works on. Calculate your company's overhead cost per hour (total overhead divided by the number of revenue producing or billable hours) and the net profit per hour (total net profit divided by the number of hours on that project) for each project.
- Make sure that all of your projects earn the net profit per hour that you want them to earn. If there are some teams that are not achieving that net profit per hour, find out why. If you can fix the issues, then do so. If not, find another team that can do the work and achieve the net profit per hour you desire.

27.

MY BOOKKEEPER OPENED ANOTHER COMPANY CHECKING ACCOUNT WITHOUT MY KNOWLEDGE

I trusted my bookkeeper. She was competent. She produced accurate financial statements on time. I bragged about her to my friends and colleagues, and even my banker.

My bookkeeper usually made the bank deposits. She got to know the people in the bank really well. Occasionally I made the deposits. When I did, the tellers and branch manager always asked about her and said to say hello. I praised her whenever they asked about her.

This went on many years. The banker knew her and me. One day, unbeknownst to me, my bookkeeper went into the bank and said, "Charlie [not my real name] wants me to open up a new checking account." The checking account was in our company name. The bank had our business license and everything they needed to open the new account.

The bank never questioned it. After all, they knew my bookkeeper and me, and every time I was there I praised her work.

The bookkeeper brought back the bank account resolutions for me to sign. I never thought anything about it. I trusted my bookkeeper, she had a great relationship with the bank too. I just assumed that they needed an updated corporate resolution since it had been a really long time since I signed one. She added her name as a signer on the account later and brought the papers back to the bank. The new account was opened.

Small deposits were made into that account, nothing major that would attract attention. Over the years a lot of money went into that account, a little bit at a time. And she always took the money out of that account with checks that had her signature on it.

I didn't find out about it for a long time. One day I happened to go into the bank and my banker asked me about my second account. He noticed that it wasn't used very much and wondered why we opened it. I hid my shock and asked him what account he was talking about.

I had never seen that account! I said that I would go back and ask the bookkeeper about the account.

It turned out she had been embezzling for years, small amounts that I never noticed. When I added it up, a lot of money had been stolen.

What I learned:

- Never completely trust your bookkeeper.
- Make sure you know about any changes to your bank accounts. If you are signing something new, find out why you have to sign that document.

Implement these company procedures:

- Always look at your corporate bank accounts at least once per week. Many owners look at the bank accounts online every day. You will notice a new account popping up.
- Bookkeepers should never have check signing privileges.

28.

AN EMPLOYEE WAS USING THE COMPANY TRUCK FOR SIDE JOBS

Our company policy is no moonlighting. If an employee is caught doing side jobs, it is a reason for immediate dismissal.

One day we got a call from a person saying that our employee didn't fix the problem when he was at their home last week because the system wasn't working again.

My customer service representative asked for the customer's address, and she could find no record that our company personnel were at her home last week.

The person was insistent that someone was there. She explained that he was in our company truck and used our company's invoices and our company's materials from the truck.

My CSR was quick and thought to ask, "Who did you make the check out to?" Her answer: "I paid in cash. He told me he could give me a discount if I paid in cash."

Something was definitely wrong. I went to her home and looked at the invoice my employee had left. Our company logo was on the invoice. I recognized the handwriting on the invoice.

I apologized to the homeowner and said, "The company has no knowledge of the repair. This employee was probably doing unauthorized work. How did you happen to call us?"

She said, "I had a problem so I searched the Internet. I liked your company's website, and when I called I got an answering service. I left a message with them and your employee called back quickly. He was nice, asked what was happening, and explained the charges to come to my home. I said yes."

I knew that my employee was taking our work and pocketing the money.

What did I do? I had an employee fix the customer's system and fired the employee for moonlighting.

What I learned:

- Whether or not my company actually got paid for the work, the customer thought it was our company, so I have to honor the work and fix the problem.
- I enforced the company policy of no moonlighting. I fired the employee despite the fact that he was a productive employee. It hurt losing his revenues until we replaced him. However, I needed to send a message to the other employees that I meant what was written in the employee handbook.

Implement these company procedures:

- If you use an answering service to handle calls in the evenings and weekends, that service should give you a list of all calls they received and took messages for during that time period.

Give this report to a manager who is responsible for making sure that the company got paid for the work it did, even on weekends.

- Enforce company policies, even when it hurts to lose an employee. It sends a message to the remaining employees that the company is serious about enforcement and is fair to all employees.

29.

AN EMPLOYEE WAS STEALING CASH FROM THE CASH REGISTER

I operate a restaurant. I've been in the restaurant business for a long time, so I know my average revenue and food cost per ticket. We are busiest during breakfast and lunch, although we are open for dinner.

Since we provide great food at low prices, many of our customers pay us in cash. The cash register is usually full after the breakfast and after the lunch crowds have eaten. We take most of the cash out after each busy time and put it in a safe until I can go to the bank.

All of the waitresses have access to the cash register. Each can process a patron's check. Each waitress tears off the strip at the bottom of the check so she knows and we know the food and tip revenue for each customer.

One of the newer waitresses seemed to make a lot of mistakes. She added up the tickets wrong or gave the customer the wrong amount of change. We pointed out the mistakes, and she became more accurate. Within a few weeks we didn't find any mistakes.

However, I did start noticing that occasionally a ticket would be missing. The missing ticket, when we looked at the kitchen backup, showed that food was ordered on it. So, a customer must have ordered food and paid for it. Where was the cash?

This didn't happen every day, so maybe someone just made a mistake. But it happened again. I noticed it was the same waitress who had the missing tickets and the missing cash. She had to be taking the cash.

It wasn't much and it wasn't very often, but I had to find out. I started watching. Sure enough, one day I saw her pocket a ticket and the cash associated with it. She never put the money in the cash register. I let it go. The second time I saw her do it, I fired her on the spot.

What I learned:

- Watching cash is critical. Since we are a cash-based business, we must track our tickets every day. This proves that the time I take to track pays off. Had I not paid attention for months, I might have lost thousands of dollars.

Implement these company procedures:

- Always track cash payments. Have a system for entering purchases and match the purchases to the payments. It takes some time to do this, especially if you are doing it manually, but it is critical, because it is tempting to take cash.
- If you find a mistake, investigate it immediately. Then watch to see whether the mistake is corrected. You are sending a message that you are watching to all employees.

30.

SOMEONE STOLE OUR EMPLOYEE TRAVEL MONEY

Our company does a lot of work for which employees must travel to do that work. The employees use company trucks to drive to the customers' locations. They leave early Monday mornings and return on Friday evenings.

There is a meeting every Monday morning to discuss that week's work. At the end of the meeting, the employees load their trucks with the materials they need and get meal money for that week. Employees are given cash for their food expenses. Hotel and gasoline expenses are taken care of through company credit cards.

The reason we gave employees cash was, quite frankly, that I don't trust the employees with a company credit card. I prefer to give them a daily meal stipend, and most of the employees live from paycheck to paycheck. They don't have personal credit cards that they could use and get reimbursed.

The bookkeeper goes to the bank each Friday to withdraw the cash required for the following week. She puts it in a secure location in our building. The cash withdrawn can be hundreds to thousands of dollars, depending on the out-of-town work the following week.

This company travel expense procedure is well known among our employees. Everyone knows there is a lot of money in the building over the weekend.

One Monday morning when the operations manager went to get the cash, it was gone. Someone had broken in to the office during the weekend and had taken the money.

It caused a great disruption that week. I never found out who took the money.

Once that happened, our procedure changed. Soon after this happened, reloadable debit cards became available. It was the perfect solution.

Now employees receive a specific amount of money on their debit card each week, and the company just keeps $200 or less in petty cash in the building.

What I learned:

- Keeping large amounts of cash in the building was dangerous and tempting. Since everyone knew the Monday morning procedure, it was very easy for someone to plan to steal the cash.

Implement these company procedures:

- Whenever practical, never keep large amounts of cash in your office. It is too tempting for someone to steal it.
- If you do need large amounts of cash on hand, don't have the same weekly routine for getting it and storing it. That becomes easy to steal because many people will know the routine cash procedure.

31.

THE BANK SAID WE MADE A DEPOSIT ERROR

I pride myself on being accurate. I always check my work and don't make mistakes very often. I'm embarrassed when I do and feel terrible. I try to avoid these feelings.

Our company gets many checks and a little cash in the door every day. Our bank deposits are often an inch or more thick with cash and checks.

When preparing the deposit, I count the cash twice and list every check on the deposit slip. Most times there are more than one deposit slip. I back up my addition with an adding machine tape. I check the amounts against the amount that I entered into the adding machine.

Then as an additional backup, I copy all of the checks, cash, and deposit slips. When I get the receipt from the bank, I staple the receipt to the adding machine tape and copies of the checks, cash, and deposit slips.

I am confident that the deposit amount is correct.

One day the company got a notice from the bank that they were debiting our account for about $8,000 because there was a mistake on the deposit.

No way! I went back to the deposit in question and added all of the checks and cash from the deposit slip. It was right. In addition, I found the copy of the check that exactly matched the amount that the bank was debiting our account.

I took all of my backup to the bank. I showed them the deposit slip and the copies of all the checks and cash. I showed them my adding machine tape matching the amount on the deposit slip. I showed them the copy of the check for the exact amount of the debit.

This was proof that we deposited that check. The bank made the error. Somewhere and somehow they lost the check. It wasn't a mistake on my part. They credited our company's bank account for the amount of the check.

What I learned:

- Even though I had copied checks and cash for years, sometimes I wondered why I took the time to do this. What happened gave me the reason why I do this. If I didn't have copies of the checks, the bank would have said they were right and the company would have lost more than $8,000, a significant loss.

Implement this company procedure:

- Always make an adding machine tape of your deposit and copy the cash and checks that make up the deposit. Yes, this takes time. However, it could prove that your addition was right. Banks do make mistakes. You don't want them making a mistake with your money.

32.

I HAD TO GENERATE $14,352 TO PAY FOR ONE HOUR OF WASTED OVERTIME A WEEK

I noticed that one of my employees always had an hour or two of overtime every week. There never was a good reason for the overtime. I decided to find out what this hour of overtime was really costing me.

I was shocked at how much revenue the company has to generate just to pay for one hour of overtime for this employee each week.

This employee was paid $16 per hour. One hour of overtime at time and a half was $24 per hour or $1,248 per year. Then I had to add payroll taxes and worker's compensation costs to that amount. Other paid benefits, such as health insurance, are not dependent on hours worked. They are a fixed cost each month that is accounted for in the 40 hours of regular time paid each week.

The cost for payroll taxes and worker's compensation insurance are 15% of the hourly rate for our office employees. The real cost for the office employee is $1,248 plus 15% of $1,248 or $1,435.

That didn't seem like a lot. However, I then calculated the revenues the company needed to generate to pay that one hour of overtime. Our company goal is a minimum of 10% net operating profit. That meant the revenue the company had to generate to cover that one hour of overtime for the office employee is $14,352!

I started looking at all of the overtime that the company paid and realized how much it was really costing us. I cut out all overtime. Now it has to be approved by that employee's manager. And of course, I trained the managers on how much an hour of overtime really costs. They make sure that hour of overtime is justified.

What I learned:

- Overtime is expensive. It must be justified. I pay close attention to any overtime that I see on payroll checks. I want to know why it was necessary. Sometimes the managers think I am just being picky. However, by paying attention to it, overtime is minimal.

Implement these company procedures:

- Calculate the revenue you need to generate to pay for one hour of overtime. Of course, if by paying that one hour of overtime each week you can generate the additional revenues, you should gladly pay it.
- If your office employees are paid on a salary basis, you may still have to pay overtime. Check with the Department of Labor in your state.
- Look at your payroll each week. If your employees are consistently receiving an hour or

two of overtime each week, make them justify the additional hours. They might have gotten used to the additional money and are finding a way to stretch their time to receive that extra income each month.

Author's note:

Cutting hours may also increase productivity. One company owner cut all of his office employees' time from 40 hours per week to 30 hours per week when the economy turned down. He was amazed that the same amount of work was getting accomplished in those 30 hours per week that had been accomplished in the previous 40 hours per week. At that point he realized how much his employees had been stretching their time. They had been unproductive for 10 hours per week, or 25% of the time that he had previously paid them for.

Whether you pay hourly or by salary, overtime is expensive and often not worth the expense. In most cases your employees should be able to complete their work in the 40 regular hours each week.

33.

MY EMPLOYEE WAS USING OUR OFFICE DEPOT CREDIT CARD FOR PERSONAL PURCHASES

Our company has several credit cards for places where we buy things we need for our business. Office Depot is one of them.

There is only one Office Depot credit card, and I keep it in the bookkeeper's office. Then, when we need office supplies, an employee gets the credit card from the bookkeeper, buys the supplies, and brings the credit card and receipt back. The bookkeeper is supposed to review the receipt and enter the purchase into our accounting software. It turned out she wasn't looking at the receipts and statements carefully. After all, she was busy, and these were small purchases and a small detail.

Many times the purchases are made on the way home, because the employee drives right past Office Depot to get to her house.

One evening an employee picked up the Office Depot credit card and made the purchases on her way home. The next morning she brought the office supplies in from her car and gave the bookkeeper the receipt.

I happened to be in the bookkeeper's office when she brought the receipt in. It looked right. I asked to see the last statement just as a check against the receipts. There were charges on the statement that did not have backup receipts.

Then I started pulling other Office Depot statements and supporting receipts. There was a pattern. Every time this employee went to purchase supplies for the company she always had one or two additional personal items on a separate receipt.

I fired her immediately and gave the bookkeeper a strong warning. It was her responsibility to receive the receipts but also verify that the company receipts were the only receipts on the statement.

What I learned:

- You have to look at the receipts, not only the total. The bookkeeper was busy and the total didn't seem too out of line, so she just let it pass.

Implement this company procedure:

- If you have company credit cards, whenever an employee uses a credit card for a company purchase, verify that purchase. When the statements come in at the end of the month, verify that all purchases on that statement have receipts for what was purchased. Question things that don't make sense. Employees will be less likely to try to put their own purchases on company credit cards if they know you are watching.

34.

MY EMPLOYEE WAS CONSTANTLY GETTING PERSONAL PHONE CALLS

In my company, employees used their own cell phones. We did not supply cell phones to employees until the personal phone calls during company paid time became excessive. Here is what happened.

One of my crews never completed its projects in the estimated time to complete the job. Other crews occasionally missed deadlines, but this crew rarely made a deadline.

I started going to the job sites unannounced. I observed where the crew couldn't see me but I could see them. I announced myself when I was ready and had observed the activity. Every time I went to a job site I saw a senior member of the team on his cell phone.

When I asked the other crew members about it, they concurred. His phone rang constantly. Sometimes it was his girlfriend. Other times it was his mother or another member of his family.

"Why didn't you tell me?" I asked.

None of the junior members felt comfortable "ratting" on a senior member of the crew. It just wasn't done.

I met with that team leader. I told him what I had observed and asked him to tell his family members not to call him at work unless it was an emergency. He was a leader and other members of the team would follow his behavior. If he was taking personal phone calls on the job, it sent a signal that it was OK for them to take personal calls too.

His team's productivity was low and needed to increase. I told him the reason I thought it was low was because of all the personal calls. If the productivity didn't come up, I would have to split up his crew and replace him.

I also told him that I would be issuing company phones and those were the only ones to be answered during work time. He didn't have to use his personal phone for company business anymore.

The phone calls stopped for a while. Then they became texts. Productivity never increased. The crew was split up and the team leader was replaced.

What I learned:

- I couldn't ask employees not to use their personal cell phones during the day because they received business calls on their personal cell phones. When I issued everyone mobile phones, I could require that the company cell phone be used for business calls only and that no personal calls were to be taken on any cell phone during work hours unless it was an emergency.

Implement these company procedures:

- Always issue company mobile phones if your employees take business calls during the day. Salespeople definitely need a company phone. Then you can see the types of calls received on that mobile phone.

- If you reimburse employees for company use of personal cell phones, you are never sure which calls are business and which are personal. It can become a nightmare and a waste of time to decipher which calls are business and which calls are personal.

35.

COMPANY GAS EXPENSES WERE OUT OF CONTROL

We have a fleet of trucks. Each driver signs our vehicle policy manual, which includes safe driving requirements, truck maintenance and repair procedures, and limitations on use of the company gasoline credit card.

Drivers usually fill their gas tanks once per day. Occasionally on long drives, the gas tank is filled more than once per day.

A spare credit card was kept in the office for emergencies. It was rarely used.

Drivers are supposed to turn in their receipts for fuel purchases. Unfortunately we were lax in enforcing this procedure and we never got all of the receipts.

Then we decided that each time the vehicle was filled with gasoline, the driver would called the office with the mileage on the truck rather than enforcing the receipt procedure.

This actually was worse, because we didn't get any of the receipts. The bookkeeper just paid the company fuel bill when it arrived. She couldn't check the statement with each credit card number's purchases.

The fuel bill started increasing. I thought that it was because revenues were increasing. So, I let it go.

One day I happened to open the mail and saw the fuel bill statement. Our emergency credit card was being used frequently. Sometimes there were two purchases in a single day for trucks I knew were not traveling far.

I found that one of the accounting employees had the emergency card and was using it for her personal vehicle. Some employees were filling up their personal vehicles on the company credit card too.

I fired the accounting clerk using the emergency card and told the bookkeeper to start balancing the gas card statement against required receipts. If the bookkeeper didn't have a receipt, the employees paid for the gasoline as a payroll deduction for all missing receipts (I made them sign an authorization for this; they weren't happy but they did it).

Finally I found a credit card company that required inputting the gas mileage before gas could be dispensed into a vehicle. When the trucks went in for maintenance, we checked the mileage against the gasoline receipt mileages. We made sure the two mileages were close.

What I learned:

- If you think expenses are increasing, delve into those expenses. My gut told me they were. I ignored it for a while. I just happened to see the statement in the mail that started the investigation. Had I not seen it, the personal use of company fuel credit cards would have gone on for a long time.

Implement these company procedures:

- Always balance your credit card statements against receipts. If receipts are missing, find out why.
- Many companies implement a "no receipt, no payment" policy. It ensures that you get the receipts. Look at them to make sure they are legitimate. Yes, it takes time. However, it is your hard-earned cash that could be paying for employees' personal expenses.

Author's note:

There were many stories similar to this form of theft. One company went so far as to have a gasoline tank installed in its yard. Trucks came to the building to fill up their tanks. If they were driving out of town, they were issued a gasoline credit card for that trip. It was returned when the driver returned to the area.

36.

MY VENDOR WAS DOING SIDE JOBS WITH MY EMPLOYEE

Our company has relationships with many vendors who supply us with materials. Our employees have the authority to purchase materials. Whenever they purchase materials they are required to give the vendor a purchase order number, and the vendor is supposed to give them the price for the materials purchased.

Each project is given an internal project number, and this project number must appear on the purchase order.The bookkeeper matches purchase orders, receipt of materials, and the invoice before a bill is paid.

One day the company received a bill for materials that had no information. We couldn't track it. We couldn't find any project that this material was supposedly purchased for.

When we called the accounting department for the vendor, the vendor told us it was ordered and picked up by one of our employees and that payment was due for this material.

We told them that there is no record that this material was authorized and that we weren't paying for it. (We spend a lot of money with this vendor.) It became a problem.

We asked the vendor for a list of all material purchases for the past three months. We found material purchases that were paid with cash that never hit our monthly statement. All of these purchases were made by one employee. Something was wrong.

We confronted the employee. He had made a side deal with one of the employees of the vendor. He paid cash using our account as authorization for these purchases. The one we caught slipped through the cracks. He hadn't paid for it yet and the materials ended up on our statement.

We fired him immediately. It hurt because he was a productive, valued employee. We then went to vendor's owner and told him what happened and we were not paying for that material.

This material purchase was removed from our statement. To our knowledge, their employee who made the side deal was not fired.

What I learned:

- You have to fire someone for stealing, even if it hurts. It took several months to replace this employee. However, the message must be sent and enforced so that other employees learn from the incident.
- Stand up for what is right. If this vendor had forced us to pay for the materials that we didn't authorize and there was proof that this was happening, we would have found another vendor and stopped using them.

Implement these company procedures:

- Always require project or job numbers on any purchase order for materials. This way you can track these numbers and know all materials purchased for that project.

- Review your statements from your vendors. Make sure that material purchases have a purchase order number, a packing slip showing the materials were received, and that the price on the purchase order is the price on the invoice before the bill is paid.

37.

THEY CAN'T BE STEALING FROM ME—I HAVE CAMERAS WATCHING

My company has a huge warehouse with about $500,000 in inventory in it at all times. We have the revenues to support that amount of inventory, and it turns over very quickly.

Since there so much inventory the temptation to steal is there. So, I installed cameras in the warehouse to prevent this potential issue.

We know our job costs and track our purchases. We also know our gross margins well. Our accounting system and books are clean, and I get a financial statement, which I review, once a month.

This statement also goes to an outside consultant, who analyzes the statements and reports back.

One month the gross margin was lower than expected. What was going on? It might have been a one-month glitch that would reverse itself the next month. I never dreamed someone was stealing from me.

The next month the gross margin was again lower than it should be. Material purchases seemed higher than they should be. Again, I thought that someone was just not accounting for materials properly.

My outside consultant also saw this and sent me an email after the second month: "Someone is stealing inventory."

I emailed back: "No way. We have cameras in the warehouse, and I didn't see anything unusual."

It turned out that someone was stealing from me. The only place in the warehouse that didn't have video surveillance was right by the back door. I started watching.

One night I caught two employees taking materials out the back door and through the fence. They had cut a hole in the chain-link fence and put it back together so that someone driving by would never see it.

Unbeknownst to anyone I put cameras in the yard and by the back door of the warehouse. I caught them and had them arrested.

What I learned:

- If your gross margins are well known, and they are not where they are supposed to be, something is wrong.
- I thought that I had everything covered with the cameras. I was wrong. Someone found a way around them and stole from me. Nothing is ever 100% foolproof.

Implement these company procedures:

- Get your financial statements on time every month. If something seems wrong one month, and you can't find the reason, sometimes it does reverse itself the next month. If it doesn't, you must find the issue and resolve it.
- Cameras in offices and warehouses are becoming common and should be considered. It

may not be employees stealing, but outsiders coming into your office or warehouse. If you can see them on a camera, you have a better chance of catching them.

COMPANY CASH PROCEDURES

These stories demonstrate how small business owners handle cash.

38.

I WAS LOSING A NICKEL FOR EVERY DOLLAR I GENERATED

I had the desire to start my own business. A colleague I was working with did too. We decided to become partners. Jack (not his real name) and I ventured out and began. We were very good at what we did, and the jobs started flowing in. We hired some employees, who we trained to be good at producing the work. Our employees helped us get a great reputation for doing quality work. More jobs came to us. We hired and trained more employees. The company grew.

We didn't pay too much attention to our financial statements. The CPA was supposed to do that. He asked us questions about inventory and job costs, and we guessed. We didn't have time to delve into those unimportant things. Our profit and loss statement, provided to us by our CPA using the figures we gave him, showed that the company was profitable. The CPA never questioned the information we gave him to compile our financial statements and taxes.

We thought the company was growing and we were paying attention to our customers. As long as we had the cash to do what we wanted to do and all of the bills were paid, we were doing great.

The company grew to about $2 million in revenues and stopped growing. We were stable at that level of sales and comfortable with managing the number of employees needed to produce that $2 million. We started noticing that it became harder and harder to pay all of the bills. We didn't have the cash flow that we used to have. Something was wrong.

We hired an industry consultant to help us determine what was wrong. At the end of the analysis, we discovered that once overhead was taken into consideration, our company was losing five cents for every dollar it took in the door.

How could that be? We guessed at inventory. We gave a number to our CPA each year to include on our taxes without actually counting it. We had no clue about material shrinkage and job cost. That was our undoing. These guesses were what caused the profit and loss statement to have a positive bottom line rather than showing a loss.

The consultant explained that growth masks many problems. The cash from one job started the next job. As long as the company was growing, sufficient cash was collected to pay the bills from that job and start the next job. Since the loss was "only a nickel," when we stopped growing it took a while to start seeing that the company was having problems paying its bills. Our growth hid the cash shortages.

We were lucky that we had a great reputation and were able to raise our prices to cover the shortfall. Several of our customers also remarked that they could never understand how we could provide quality work as cheap as we had been doing it.

What I learned:

- Having cash does not mean that you are profitable. We didn't pay enough attention to knowing what our costs were to truly understand whether the company was profitable.

- Have a CPA who questions the information you give him. Since he didn't question anything, we never knew that we could be giving him wrong information.
- Don't guess on inventory. Track it carefully, since inventory losses can cause a job to be unprofitable.
- Know your costs of doing business. We didn't consider overhead in our pricing. We just guessed at it. After all, we had enough cash to pay all of our bills, including inventory costs.

Implement these company procedures:

- Know the total cost for performing a job. This includes the direct cost for labor and materials as well as the indirect overhead costs. Make sure that each job you quote is profitable before you begin work.
- Count inventory each year so you will have an accurate figure for your balance sheet and your taxes. You can see what the shrinkage, if any, was. If there was shrinkage, take steps to track it carefully.
- Have a great reputation for doing quality work. Price increases, if they are small, can usually be enacted without all of your customers looking for another supplier.

39.

BE YOUR OWN LINE OF CREDIT

I sat in one of Ruth King's seminars in the 1990s. She told us that we could become our own line of credit and didn't have to spend sleepless nights worrying about payroll and paying our bills. I paid attention.

The process was simple. Every time you get a payment from a customer, whether it is cash, check, or credit card, you take 1% of that payment and put it in a savings account.

I decided to do it. I instructed my bookkeeper to put 1% of every bank deposit in the company's savings account. This way I could watch the savings grow. And it did.

Fast forward about 20 years. I was in another of Ruth King's seminars where she talked about saving 1% of all revenues. I raised my hand and said to the group, "This works. This is what happened to me. In 2008 when the economy tanked, the building next to my building came up for sale. It was incredibly cheap because the owner needed money. I had the money in my savings account because I had been putting the 1% away. I thought that perhaps the company would need it for expansion. I didn't have to go to the bank to borrow money to buy the building. I wrote a check. I recently sold the building and made a good profit."

What I learned:

- You never know when you will need cash in your savings account for business expenses or when an opportunity might come your way. Over the years I have become my own line of credit. Whenever I need cash for payroll or another business purchase, I have it. If I use it, I always repay the savings account when extra cash comes in the door.

Implement these company procedures:

- Put 1% of collected revenues in a savings account. Every time you make a bank deposit, take 1% of that deposit and put it in a savings account. If your savings account is at the same bank as your operating account, it is easy to transfer money between the two accounts. Fair warning: It's easy to take money out too. Don't be tempted to take the money for nonbusiness purposes. You never know when an opportunity will come your way. If you save the 1% you could have the cash to take advantage of the opportunity.
- If you use money from the savings account, always repay it when extra cash comes in the door. This is the only way to ensure that cash is available when you might need it.

Author's note:

Over the years I have received emails and letters from business owners who have implemented this strategy. All thank me and tell me stories about how they had the money to handle business crises and to purchase assets needed for operations or opportunities such as in this story. Put the 1% away!

40.

I FOUND A CHECK FLOATING IN THE PARKING LOT

I was walking into my building one morning and noticed a piece of paper fluttering in the wind. I decided to investigate that piece of paper. It was a check from a customer.

I was surprised. I wasn't sure whose work the check was from. I decided to do nothing. I put the check in my desk and waited to see what would happen.

Sure enough, a few days later my bookkeeper came to me and said that a check was missing from a service ticket. The service technician swore that he got the check from the customer and turned it in with his paperwork. As proof, he said that, as usual, he put the check number on his service ticket when the customer gave it to him.

The dispatcher, who received the paperwork, swore that she didn't get it. The bookkeeper didn't feel comfortable calling the customer and ask whether she paid the bill because the technician had written the check number on the service ticket. What should she do?

I pulled the check out of my drawer and handed it to her. I told her that I saw the check floating around in the parking lot. I also talked to the service manager to ensure that this would never happen again.

All of the field personnel got staplers. They were to staple cash and checks to their service tickets. When the dispatcher received the paperwork, she was to put her initials on the paperwork indicating that she had received the payment. She was to do this in front of the employee turning in his paperwork.

Since credit card payments are done through a credit card reader and approved in the field, these payments automatically go into our checking account. The technician simply writes the approval number on the service ticket.

Now payments received in the field don't get lost.

What I learned:

- I wanted to see how honest our bookkeeper and office staff were. They didn't disappoint me. They followed procedure and told me of a problem.
- This incident showed me that our cash and check receiving procedures were too loose. We tightened them up and ensured that everyone receiving cash and checks signed off that they had received them. The staplers ensured that the field employees didn't have a loose check flying around in their vans or stuck in between the seats.

Implement these company procedures:

- Whenever payments are received from field employees, the person receiving them must initial the paperwork that the payments were received by that person. This way you can track the money trail if there is a problem.

- Using staplers is easy. All payments should be attached to the paperwork accompanying that payment. Paper clips don't work because they can come off.

41.

MY SALESPERSON GOT $8,000 IN CASH

Our policy is that when a project is completed, the salesperson goes to the business, reviews the work, and collects payment for the work. This is written into our contracts and is standard policy unless a different payment schedule is negotiated.

The company performed work for a restaurant under our standard payment policy. At the end of the project, the salesperson went to the restaurant to review the work with the owner and collect payment.

The owner of the restaurant was satisfied with our work. When the salesperson asked for a check, the owner gave him $8,000 in a brown paper bag. The salesperson noted the payment on the invoice, signed it, and gave the restaurant owner a copy of the paid invoice.

The salesperson left quickly, got in his car, and called the office. He was nervous because he was carrying $8,000. What should he do?

I found out about it from the person who answered his call. I called him back and told him to go to the bank. I would have someone meet him there with a deposit slip. I didn't want $8,000 lying around the office tempting anyone.

The salesperson met our bookkeeper at the bank. She had a deposit slip, and the money was put in our operations account immediately. The bookkeeper also got the paid invoice from the salesperson so she could enter the payment into our accounting system.

What I learned:

- You never know when a customer will give you a large amount of cash as payment. I knew that this was too much cash for anyone to carry around. I also knew that the salesperson was nervous carrying around that much money; I could hear it in his voice. It's important that the cash goes into your operations checking account for safekeeping as quickly as possible.

Implement these company procedures:

- Establish the maximum amount of cash any person can have at one time. Anytime anyone has more than the maximum amount, he is to bring the cash to the office or for larger amounts, as in this story, call the office and someone will meet that person at the bank with a deposit slip.
- Either way, no employee should be responsible for carrying large amounts of company cash, and the employees shouldn't want the liability of doing so either.

42.

CASH OR ACCRUAL ACCOUNTING?

Our CPA compiled our taxes on a cash basis, so I assumed that the company should operate on a cash basis too. I had no clue what cash accounting or accrual accounting was.

I never printed a balance sheet because I didn't know what they were for and didn't think it would have any information that would be useful to me. I looked at my profit and loss statement and it said that we were profitable. That's all I cared about.

We began having cash flow problems, which I didn't understand because my profit and loss statement said that the company was profitable. So, I started looking for help.

I stumbled on an explanation of cash versus accrual accounting and found out that I would almost always be profitable in cash basis accounting because the only time we paid bills was when we had the cash to do so.

I asked my accountant about switching to accrual accounting, and he said that I could do it. So, I switched the accounting system to accrual basis and was shocked. Our company was losing money. Our pricing was wrong, and we weren't charging enough.

The accrual accounting showed me accounts receivable and accounts payable, so I knew what all of our expenses really were, and I could match revenues against expenses each month. This is how I discovered that we weren't charging enough.

Now I look at everything on an accrual basis and let my CPA prepare my taxes on a cash basis.

What I learned:

- Cash accounting is fine for tax purposes, but it isn't a good way to look at a business on a day-to-day basis.
- Accrual accounting is a much more accurate way to look at our business on a day-to-day basis. It truly tells me what is occurring with accounts payable and accounts receivable.

Implement this company procedure:

- For operational purposes, most businesses must operate on an accrual basis. There are three major reasons why. First, most businesses have accounts receivable. Watch accounts receivable on a monthly basis to ensure that the company is getting paid promptly. Second, most businesses have accounts payable. Watch accounts payable to make sure that the company has the cash to take discounts where appropriate and to pay bills promptly. Third, to properly match sales and expenses against sales, the business needs to operate on an accrual basis. Otherwise gross margins will vary widely, depending on when the company receives the cash for products and services it produced and pays the expenses incurred to produce these products and services. A consistent gross margin is critical for financial management. The best way to monitor actual costs as compared to bids is to look at the company's gross margin. Consistency requires that the company operate on an accrual basis.

Author's note:

Cash accounting records a sale when you get paid for the sale, not when you give the invoice to the customer. An expense is recorded when you pay the bill. There are no accounts receivable and accounts payable.

Accrual accounting records a sale when you send an invoice to the customer, whether or not you have been paid. An expense is recorded when you receive the invoice for the expense, not when you pay the bill. There are accounts receivable and accounts payable.

43.

WATCH WHAT YOU SIGN

I had someone sitting in my office while I was signing payroll checks. We were talking about business issues. Suddenly I started laughing. My manager asked what was so funny since we were discussing something serious.

I handed him the payroll check. He started laughing too, imagining what would have happened had we not caught the mistake.

The payroll check had an extra zero in the amount. Instead of $1,235 it was written for $12,350. It was an honest mistake by the bookkeeper. At least I thought it was.

"Can you imagine what would have happened if this employee had gotten this check?" the manager asked.

"He would have gone to the bank, cashed the check, and said nothing. He then would have gone on a buying spree. We never would have gotten the money back unless we took it from payroll deductions each week. And it would have taken a long time to get it back."

After our discussion, I brought the signed checks and the wrong check to the bookkeeper. I asked him whether payroll balanced that week. He said that it seemed a little high but couldn't find anything wrong. I showed him the check with the extra zero. He turned bright red and apologized immediately. I knew that he was embarrassed for making that mistake.

By watching what I signed we prevented an employee from getting cash that he didn't earn and potentially never getting it back. The bookkeeper never made another payroll mistake. It was an honest error.

What I learned:

- Mistakes do happen. This was an honest mistake that the bookkeeper made. Since I sign all of my checks, I saw the mistake, even though I was in conversation with a manager.
- I remembered why I instituted the "I sign all checks" policy when this happened. It was a great reminder.

Implement these company procedures:

- Sign all of the checks and watch what you sign. Signature stamps are dangerous and can lead to theft.
- If something doesn't look right, put the check aside and ask for backup before you sign it.

44.

I GAVE MY BOOKKEEPER CHECK SIGNING AUTHORITY

I travel a lot for business. Our company has clients all over the United States, and I visit them frequently. Since I am not in the office much, I gave check signing authority to my bookkeeper. She signs many of the checks to pay bills and handles the accounts for our company.

I do look at the financial statements each month and have questioned numbers in the past. She always had backup supporting the expenses, so I relaxed and stopped paying attention to the minute details.

That was my mistake. I think that the embezzlement began a few years after she started working for the company. By that point I trusted her financial statements and wasn't asking many questions anymore. The checks I saw signed looked legitimate since they were to vendors.

It never was large amounts, a few hundred dollars here and there. Then new vendors appeared. Checks written to them were never large amounts and the expenses looked legitimate. I never thought to ask for backup. I trusted her.

I guess she hit her limit on the amount she wanted to steal because one day she just didn't come to work. She disappeared. I couldn't reach her on her home phone or her cell phone. I thought it was really strange and was worried that something had happened to her.

I hired another bookkeeper. This is when the embezzlement came to light. We found the fake vendors and checks that were written to herself. The checks to herself were never big. But they were consistent and frequent. The embezzlement amounted to tens of thousands of dollars over the time period.

Since I gave her check signing authority, she could write the checks to herself. Had I not given her the ability to sign checks, this may not have happened. Or, unfortunately, she would probably have found another way to steal cash from our company.

What I learned:

- Never give your bookkeeper check signing authority. Had she forged the checks, I could have prosecuted her criminally. Since I gave her the ability to write checks, she did. And they were not always checks to pay company bills.
- I look at the bank statement now before I give it to the new bookkeeper to balance the checkbook. In addition, even when I am out of town, I look at my cash balance every day. I want to know what has been written against our account. I'm watching more closely, even though I'm not in the office.
- Checks have to wait to be signed until I return from my out-of-town trips. The new bookkeeper cannot sign checks.

Implement these company procedures:

- Only company owners should have check signing privileges.
- Send your bank statements home. This is the first line of defense in keeping the honest people honest. Look at the pictures of your checks and make sure that they are yours and are written for the proper amount.
- Bookkeepers should not want check signing privileges. If taxes are not paid, the bookkeeper is liable for them because she has check signing privileges.

WAYS TO RAISE CASH QUICKLY

These last stories describe what some small business owners did to raise cash quickly when they faced cash shortages.

45.

I DID WHAT I TELL MY CLIENTS TO DO— AND IT WORKED

I started my consulting and coaching practice to help small business owners grow their business. I was successful selling and delivering, and very soon I found myself in that feast-or-famine mode: I got so busy delivering that I forgot to keep selling.

One of my customers, who paid me $80,000, came to the conclusion that our work was done. On my way out the door it occurred to me that I had to replace that revenue. How was I going to do that?

When I started my business I started with a Rolodex. I found that I exhausted that Rolodex and referrals from that Rolodex within 12 months. I didn't proactively sell and market. I was in trouble.

I sat down with my mentor at the time and said, "I'm really having trouble replacing my largest client." He just looked at me and said, "You know, there is nothing more pathetic than a growth consultant complaining about not being able to grow his own business."

As I wiped the blood off my ears I very quickly recognized that I needed to call 100 people to make 10 appointments. I needed 10 appointments to uncover three potential projects. These three project proposals invariably lead to one or two sales. So as the next 60 days went on I grew my business by $60,000 immediately and then a lot more.

I created a script that was intriguing and would entice prospective customers to call back. And it worked…just like the statements I create for my clients.

These phone calls lead to proposals, work, success, and more work. As time went on I started a newsletter and wrote books.

But it all really started by effectively walking my own talk. I also recognized that I have to keep the pipeline flowing when I am busy—just as I tell my clients. If I don't, I am doomed to failure.

What I learned:

- Never be afraid of picking up the telephone and asking for a referral or calling a potential customer who was referred by a current customer.
- I still have ups and downs. People are afraid to take action in good economic times and bad economic times. The key is to provoke people to recognize that they can manage their own destiny and in fact investing in their own growth is a good idea. This never really changes.

Implement these company procedures:

- The age of your business doesn't matter. Continue selling and marketing. In reality, sometimes it's the new businesses that are the ones that do it the best because they haven't developed bad habits. The trouble with being in business for many years is that you say to yourself, "Gee, I've done all this marketing, so I don't have to do the cold calls." Don't ever forget how to do it, because times change and you can't assume that what you've been doing will continue to work forever.

- Make sure that you are helping people to raise cash, cut costs, or succeed in the shortest term. People like to see a quick payback on their investment.

46.

I KNOCKED ON DOORS TO RAISE CASH

We were in a seasonal business, and February was our slowest month. I saved some money from operations during the rest of the year, but it never seemed to be enough to cover February's overhead.

I had to do something to bring revenues in the door to cover the company's expenses. I had never been afraid of cold calling. I learned it trading bonds for two years. I sat in a room with about 50 salespeople who worked a telephone all day. I learned that if you sell something, you make something. And I did make a lot of money. I saw what sales was all about, and I watched successful salespeople. Just by watching I developed a good psychology about what it would take to be successful at sales.

I took the experience of sitting in a boiler room on the telephone all day and translated it into knocking on homeowners' doors. It took a while to get good at it. However, I persisted and became successful.

I got a lot of rejection. However, one or two people agreed to an appointment, which I set for later. I never knocked on doors and sold at the same time. I didn't think that was a good idea. I needed time to get to know the homeowner, and I couldn't do it just knocking on their door. Setting the appointment for a later time was the way to go.

By knocking on doors every day I generated the revenues I needed to keep my company alive in

February. Whenever the telephone wasn't ringing, I went out canvassing neighborhoods for sales.

Eventually I taught a team of five salespeople how to do this. They resisted at first, but those who learned the technique made a lot of money.

What I learned:

- I needed to generate sales since the sales were not coming in the door. Cold calling in neighborhoods worked. I was familiar with a form of it from my bond sales days, and I applied what I had learned to keep my company alive.
- Once you perfect a skill, teach it to others. Other people can be taught to do what you do, which frees you up to work on the business.

Implement this company procedure:

- While knocking on doors may not be practical for your business, there is always something that you can do to generate sales. It might mean calling everyone you have given a proposal to who hasn't said yes. It might mean calling to ask for referrals from existing customers. It might mean going to industry or association meetings of your prospective customers and getting to know them. Or, it may be something else. The key is to do *something*. Don't sit and complain that sales are not coming in the door. Sometimes you have to make them happen.

47.

I HAD A $4 MILLION SURPRISE

Many years ago I was hired as the operations manager for a casino. It was one of my first jobs.

Surprise! The first day on the job I learned that the casino was losing about $400,000 per year and there was a $4 million tax bill that wasn't paid.

This was a cash flow nightmare. On top of this, every penny had to be counted accurately to ensure that we wouldn't be fined by the gaming commission. If we were off by even five cents, the casino would be fined. We didn't need any more bills than we already had.

It was obvious that we needed to accurately generate revenue fast at little or no cost to us. But how to do it? I was in my 20s without a lot of experience. However, I was enthusiastic and had a lot of energy. I put together a short business plan based on my limited experience.

I went to the Service Corps of Retired Executives (SCORE). I asked the organization for help from their five best volunteers. I needed input and advice from seasoned executives. These five individuals bought into the plan, made some great suggestions, and helped me implement it.

Outside-of-the-box ideas were needed to get people to the casino. I called a hot tub distributor I had worked with and asked him to provide five hot tubs and figure out a way to have them operational in the parking lot of the casino. He did, and we had a hot tub party in the middle of the winter.

We had a battle of the bands, which also generated cash flow. The bands promoted the event. I got the local Chamber of Commerce, the radio stations, and all the media in the area to promote the event. I convinced them to be sponsors, so there was little cost to the casino.

We had events every month. Each time there was an event the casino made money. The more events we had, the more people came to the casino after the event. I could see the cash flow and profitability steadily increasing.

The casino broke even in less than two years and the tax bill was paid.

What I learned:

- Having little or no money makes you very creative. I accomplished things I never could have if I had had a budget for the events.
- Ask people for help. All they can do is say no, and many will say yes if you give them a reason why they will benefit from what you are asking them to do.
- A business plan, no matter how sketchy, is important to getting through the tough times.

Implement these company procedures:

- When you get a surprise, get experienced people to help you. SCORE volunteers help because they enjoy it. However, if you don't have a SCORE chapter in your area, ask for recommendations from people you know who have dealt with extreme situations.

- Create a plan to get out of the cash flow crunch. Even if it isn't executed exactly as you wrote it, you have the goal in mind and steps to achieve it. The exact steps rarely are exactly the same as you've written them in the business plan.
- Give people a reason to get behind you. Will they increase their exposure, sales, audience, or something else? Clearly explain what you want, why you want it, and what's in it for them.

48.

WE DISCOUNTED TO RAISE CASH

We had a cash flow problem. We had significant receivables from well-established companies. We thought that we could sell the receivables (a process called factoring) and visited several factoring companies to learn about what their process was. At the end of the conversations I realized that the fees were prohibitive and would significantly cut into our profit margins even though we would get instant money through our receivables.

A day later I realized that our company could become its own factoring company. The company could discount the receivables to the client. The company gets the cash that I'm looking for, and the client gets the money that factoring company was going to get. I could increase my cash flow and help increase the profit of my customer versus the profit of the factoring company.

That is what we did. We visited a variety of our clients who had current receivables on the books. We didn't factor old receivables, but current receivables. We still continued to pursue the people who owed us money, but old money already had an effective discount because it was late, so I didn't want to discount on top of a discount.

The company continued to mail its invoices at the full amount quoted for our products and services. Customers weren't aware of the discount until a member of my staff or I notified them. We waited a week after they were billed to begin the notification process. The goal was to give them the discount if they paid the bill that week.

We literally called clients on the phone and explained what was going on. We know most of the customers we do business with. I know a lot of the owners myself, so I just called them. I explained that we were trying to raise some additional capital for some projects that we have, and that to do that we were self-funding it rather than borrowing it from the bank or factoring it. I explained further that we were willing to give them a discount equal to what we would pay in interest or to the factoring company. We explained that the discount was 5% if the customer paid the invoice this week. We were totally honest with our customers and told them we would like to pass the savings on to them. We got $27,000 in 20 days.

The clients were appreciative that we offered the discount, and they understood what we were doing. In fact, several of our clients did the same process with their clients. It has worked well for all of us.

Our company doesn't discount a net 5% on our invoices all the time. We've only used it a couple of times, because we don't want our customers to think they are always going to get a 5% discount for paying early. When we did use it we raised significant amounts of cash that we needed to get.

What I learned:

- The more honest I am with customers, especially business owners, the more my relationships seem to grow. Not everyone took advantage of the discount, but everyone appreciated the honesty. I was amazed at how many of my customers actually used this process to raise cash for their businesses.

- Being creative in ways to raise cash can actually produce long-term client relationships. Many of my customers had experienced the same issues in the past. They were pleased to see that we were addressing them creatively.

Implement these company procedures:

- Look at your credit policies and how you are extending credit. In many businesses, the policy is to give everybody credit and expend 100% of cost of goods sold. Then you must collect a receivable. As cash gets tight, you may revise the policy to request that customers prepay or pay along with the job.
- Factoring can be a viable alternative for some companies and some situations. Make sure you understand the fees and processes before you agree to use this method to raise cash.

49.

ELIMINATE YOUR ACCOUNTS RECEIVABLE

My goal is to eliminate accounts receivable for small businesses. I started NOWaccount because my customers were not paying me in the time agreed to on the contracts and my vendors wanted to get paid. Getting a loan or a line of credit was not an option.

I decided to find a way to eliminate accounts receivable. Retail stores and restaurants don't have accounts receivable, so why should most small businesses have them?

Since small businesses are the largest bank in the world, lending their customers trillions of dollars, I wanted to create a way for small businesses to eliminate their accounts receivable just as retail stores and restaurants have done.

Enter NOWaccount. These accounts are for small business owners whose customers are business to business or business to government. It isn't factoring, and there is no recourse if the customer doesn't pay us. We take the risk. The fees are about the same as you pay credit card companies when you take credit cards for payment, and you get paid in about the same amount of time: two to three days. There are no personal guarantees for payment.

This means you can sell, buy the products and materials you need to fulfill the sale, and get your money quickly.

We have helped thousands of businesses grow. They have the cash they need to hire people and give their customers extended payment terms. One customer actually gave her customers 60-day terms when other companies in the industry were giving the standard 10-day payment terms. This increased her business dramatically.

Bankers also like NOWaccount because it helps free up cash flow to pay their loans. Their customers aren't complaining that they can't pay their loan payments because their customers are not paying them.

If you are interested in NOWaccount, go to www.nowaccount.com.

The application process is quick and easy, then you can start using your account to grow your business and get paid quickly.

Author's note:

I wanted to include this story because I have personally seen how NOWaccount has helped small businesses. I first met Lara Hogdson, founder and CEO of NOWaccount, when the company was just getting off the ground. They have grown exponentially by helping many business owners eliminate their accounts receivable, Lara's personal goal.

50.

MEATBALL MARKETING

This final story gives you quick ideas to raise cash quickly.

Meatball marketing is what you do when you've got to get cash in the door fast. It's what you do when the telephone isn't ringing. It's not months of planning and thousands of dollars in expense.

Meatball marketing was coined by a marketing professional who would much rather have the luxury of time to analyze, discuss, and analyze some more before making a decision.

Alas! You don't always have the luxury of months and months of analyzing before you create a marketing campaign to send a message to your clients and attract new clients.

Even when you do create a marketing action plan for the year, you always watch to make sure that the message you are sending is appropriate.

What do I mean? If you are in the heating business, one of the marketing activities you do in the fall is promote heating system checks to make sure the furnace is in operating condition on that first cold day when it is needed.

If your geographic area is experiencing an unusually hot fall, that furnace message will be ignored. Who wants to turn on their furnace when their air-conditioning system is still needed? Better to wait until it gets cooler to send out that marketing piece.

Act fast when weather emergencies give you a gift: cleaning up after a hurricane, tornado, earthquake, or even several days of heavy rain or 100-degree scorching weather at 90% humidity. It's time for meatball marketing.

So what is meatball marketing? Getting out there and letting the world know you exist. For example, how many of your neighbors know what you do? How many companies in the industrial parks or streets where your offices are located know what you do?

A company owner was complaining about it being slow and the telephone not ringing. I told him to go to each of the companies in his industrial park and surrounding industrial parks and introduce his company. He came back with a significant project in a slower time of the year. Meatball marketing worked for him.

Two partners wanted to start an HVAC company from scratch. They were concerned about how to generate customers. The answer? Choose a neighborhood and drive your truck in that neighborhood every Saturday morning. Within a year they owned that neighborhood. Meatball marketing worked for them.

Right before the last major hurricane hit New Jersey, the owner called all of his generator clients and had them test their generators. They were thankful and appreciative of his call. It didn't cost anything but time. It was creative meatball marketing that paid dividends in loyal customers and additional work after the storm hit.

SEO is meatball marketing too. Up your ad purchases at times of the year when your potential customers are looking for your type of business to solve their needs. It might be Christmas trees in November or florists around Valentine's Day or Mother's Day.

Creating new SEO ads takes little time, and your messages can instantly appear at a time where your prospective customers are paying attention because they need you. Of course, you must have everything set up before the crisis hits so you can take advantage of it. And in slower times of the year, drop your SEO spend. People are not paying attention because they don't need you.

Invest in a sign that lets you change the messages on it weekly or monthly. People will drive by and get your message. Meatball marketing again.

What other meatball marketing tactics work? Putting your business cards on bulletin boards in grocery stores, in restaurants, or anywhere people are likely to see them. If you make them a color other than white, they will stand out on those boards.

Look for opportunities. One day I was walking my dog and a car stopped. She said, "If you ever needed dog sitting, call me" and handed me her card. Another example of meatball marketing.

Meatball marketing is being proactive rather than reactive. It is looking for opportunities. It is getting out from behind your desk and talking to people. Most will say no. However, there will be some who say yes…and increase your revenues.

What meatball marketing can you do today?

PART TWO

WHAT YOU CAN DO ABOUT IT

Which is most important: cash, cash flow, or profits?

Cash is the lifeblood of your business. Cash is critical. Without cash, you can't pay payroll and you can't keep the doors open. Without it you really don't have a business.

Is Cash Most Important?

Figure 3 shows a tank of water. Imagine that there is cash in that tank rather than water. At the beginning of the month there must be a certain level of cash in your bank accounts, even if it is a penny. You can't have negative cash: that would mean you are bouncing checks and the bank will close your account if it continues.

That's also why you can't have negative cash on your balance sheet. You've got to have at least a penny in the bank to keep your business alive.

But if cash were most important, then every month the level of cash in the tank would decrease when you paid your bills. Soon there would be no cash left and you will be out of business.

Is cash flow most important?

At the beginning of the month there is a certain level of water in the tank—that is, a certain amount of cash in the bank. Cash flow means that during the month you add to the tank of money and drain money from the tank. At the end of the month there is a certain level in the tank, which is probably different from the level that was there at the beginning of the month.

You add to the tank with cash inputs. Cash inputs are collections from sales, *not* the sale itself. You can also get cash in from selling assets, taking a loan from yourself or the bank, interest on checking and savings accounts, or investments in the business.

You open the drain on the bottom to write checks for payroll, rent, utility bills, loans, etc., and the level in the tank drops.

Figure 3

Cash flow is simply starting at the beginning of a week, month, or year and adding to it by turning the cash flow input spigot on through collections and other ways mentioned in the previous paragraph. You decrease the level in the tank by opening the cash flow drain—that is, disbursements. At the end of the week, month, or year you shut the spigot and the drain and

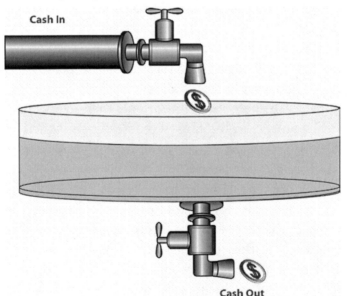

measure the level. That is the ending cash for the month

and the beginning cash for the next month.

You have a certain amount of cash to start the period. You turn the spigot on (collections on sales, loans taken out, investment income). You open the drain and out goes payroll, accounts payable payments, loan payments, etc. Level up, level down, level up, level down. There needs to be some cash in the tank—that is, cash flow must remain positive with all the income and outgo. There must be some cash when you close the spigots and the drains at the end of the month.

Don't get to a zero level. If you have a negative level or a zero level, the bank doesn't allow you to write checks. You've got to have a positive cash balance—some water in the tank—to allow checks to be written.

Cash flow is really important. Although cash is necessary to write the checks, you've got to get cash flow to get the cash to write the checks.

Are profits most important?

Profits are simply revenue minus expenses. Profits do not tell you how much cash you have. (And profitability is sustained profits month after month; year after year.)

Profit is a profit and loss statement value. Cash is a balance sheet value. They are separate and distinct.

When you get your profit and loss statement at the end of the month, the bottom line is the amount of profit you made. It is not the amount of cash you have in the bank.

You may have experienced many losing months when you had a lot of cash in the bank. There may have been other, very profitable months when your cash in the bank was low.

Profits are turned into cash when you collect your receivables and pay the bills associated with that sale.

You can be profitable and go out of business.

One former owner had been profitable for more than 10 years. In one week, three of his major customers filed bankruptcy, leaving him with more than $1 million in bad accounts receivable. He didn't have the cash to cover the expenses for those jobs and went out of business.

Another story is the one related in story 38 ("I Was Losing a Nickel for Every Dollar I Generated"). Growth masked his cash flow problems. The level of cash in the tank was rising but at 5% less than it should have. When growth stopped, the level of cash in the tank dropped 5% more than it should have every month. He was lucky that he recognized it and fixed the problem before he ran out of cash.

The answer to which is most important, cash, cash flow, or profits is: Profitable sales turn into positive cash flow, which turns into cash.

How to Watch Your Cash:
Weekly Cash Flow Report

Your weekly cash flow statement tracks cash in your business.

A cash flow statement is simply a picture of the flow of cash through your business. Figure 4 shows a weekly cash flow report.

Inputs are collections on sales. Notice it's not the sale itself. It is the collection. It's Ms. Jones's check. It's Company ABC's check. It's an employee collecting a check on a job or getting a credit card for payment. It's a customer walking into your store and giving you money for products and services they purchase. The collection of cash from the sale is critical…you need to make sales. However, if you don't collect your money, the sale doesn't count.

Other inputs might include investment income or borrowing from your bank line of credit. There might be an investment in the business (for example, an owner made a loan to the company or sold additional stock), or there might be a sale of an asset to get cash.

Inputs are cash that the company receives.

Disbursements are cash going out of the company. They are the drains on the company. Disbursements are the checks for payroll, loan payments, purchases of assets, or payment of overhead expenses.

Other disbursements might include purchases of assets or buying the stock from a stockholder. These don't happen frequently. However, they can happen.

Ending cash is just simply beginning cash plus inputs minus disbursements. Ending cash must be positive (there must be water left in the tank). Without enough cash, you need to decide who isn't getting paid, and sometimes those are the tough decisions.

Beginning cash plus cash input minus disbursements is ending cash. That is a cash flow statement.

WEEKLY CASH REPORT

Week of: _____ Prepared by: _____

Cash on hand at the beginning of the week:

Petty Cash	$
Checking Account 1	$
Checking Account 2	$
Payroll Account	$
Money Market	$
Other Savings	$
Total Beginning Cash	**$**

Cash Collected	$
CC Payments Collected	$
Accounts Rec. Collected	$
Other Inputs (Loans, etc.)	$
Total Available Cash	**$**

Disbursements:

Payroll	$
Accounts Payable	$
Loan Payments	$
Other	$
Total Disbursements	$
Total Ending Cash For Week	**$**

Estimated requirements for next week:

Accounts Rec. to be Collected	$
Payroll	$
Accounts Payable to be Paid	$
Loan Payments Due	$
Total Estimated Cash Surplus/Needs Next Week:	**$**

Now, now do you use cash flow statements? You can use them yearly, monthly, or weekly. A yearly cash flow statement doesn't do too much for you, because unless you have a crystal ball, you're not going to be able to predict on January 1 the amount of cash you have on December 31 with much accuracy.

I like weekly cash flow statements. They review what has happened during the current week and plan cash needs for the coming week.

The weekly cash flow report forces the company to be current for receivables and payables entries each week. This makes it easier to close a month and produce monthly financial statements.

The weekly cash flow statement starts with beginning cash and adds collections for the week to get a total beginning cash. Then disbursements are subtracted to get the ending cash for the week. Then I take it one step further: planning for the following week.

Estimate receivables that are going to come in, payables and loan payments that must be paid, and what payroll will be. Then take ending cash for this week and subtract payroll and disbursements for next week, and add to it expected collections for next week. The end result should be a positive number. If it's not, time must be spent on collections or deciding who isn't going to get paid.

Do these statements on Friday afternoons. If that number is negative (that is, you need more cash next week), it's a lot easier to have a week to collect that cash than to have the bookkeeper knocking on your door the day before payroll is due saying, "We don't have enough cash to make payroll."

Weekly cash reports don't take more than 15 minutes to do once the company's payables and receivables are up to date. The first one takes a little bit longer. However, once you do your first report, all subsequent reports become easier. Your ending cash for this week is your beginning cash for next week. All your bookkeeper has to do is total deposits, total disbursements, and make sure that payables and receivables are up to date so she can estimate what will come in and what needs to be paid next week.

Cash is the lifeblood of your business. Make sure that you watch your hard-earned cash!

Should I Prosecute the Thief?

Shock and disbelief are the first reactions when you uncover theft. Your thought process usually goes something like this:

1. How could this employee do this to me?
2. He/she lied to me.
3. I trusted that employee.
4. I don't believe it (until the evidence slaps you in the face).

Then, after you've gotten over the shock and disbelief, you get angry. And, if you are like most of us, you want revenge. You imagine all of the things that you will do to that person, including putting that person in jail.

Then reality hits. If an employee forged a check or stole materials, it is easier to prosecute, because it is a felony to forge a check or steal materials valued over a certain amount.

If you give your bookkeeper check signing authority, it is much harder to prosecute. It usually becomes a civil case rather than a criminal case. It can take longer and is more expensive to litigate.

Sometimes the thief says that he will repay the stolen money in return for not prosecuting him. That is a tough decision, especially if the reason for the theft was dire need (sick family member, divorce, etc.) and there are family members who can write you a check to repay the theft. He swears he learned his lesson. At the very least you *must* fire that person.

If the thief is a professional embezzler, you might decide to prosecute. After all, if this person did it to you, he probably did it to other unsuspecting small business owners. You'd be doing the small business community a favor by getting this person thrown in jail. More than likely, if the embezzler has reached the amount of money he wanted from your business, he will just disappear and you will never find him. The next person in that position finds the embezzlement.

You might decide that you learned a lesson and want it behind you. You put the procedures in place recommended in this book to keep the honest people honest. And you closely watch your processes, cash, and financial statements to foil the remaining 1% who get a perverse sense of pleasure figuring out how to steal and doing it without getting caught.

The choice is yours. It is your business, your cash, your profits. If you don't want to invest the time and money to see the prosecution to its conclusion, don't prosecute. This could take years and many thousands of dollars.

Or, if you decide to prosecute, stick with it during the tough days of a trial or a deal.

Either way, it is totally up to you.

Reporting Theft to the Internal Revenue Service

Many people think to report theft on a 1099 or W-2 form. The best place to report it is probably on IRS form 3949A. This is an information referral form for reporting potential violations of the IRS law. It is important to check with your accountant for the latest rulings, however.

As of July 2017, the month this book was written, embezzled funds are deductible in the year they are discovered. They are considered other expenses. Even if the theft has been happening for many years, the deduction is taken the year that they are discovered.

The tricky part is when you accept a repayment plan. These are taxable in subsequent years. If you charge interest, the repayment plan could be treated as a loan with interest. In these cases the repayment would be considered a reduction of debt with the interest expense reported as income.

The best thing to do is get over the embarrassment of talking with your CPA. She has probably been involved with many small business embezzlements. She can point you in the right direction with respect to reporting the embezzlement on your taxes.

Procedures to Put in Place

Protect your cash and other assets. Most important, if you aren't getting your financial statements on time or they are constantly filled with mistakes, don't accept excuses from your bookkeeper. Her job is bookkeeping! It is her responsibility to get you accurate information in a timely manner.

Usually if you don't get your financial statements on time, get computer excuses, or receive another lame excuse, the bookkeeper is incompetent or stealing from you. Decide which is happening and take action.

Cash must be controlled and monitored. Without cash your business cannot survive for long. Even if you have a profitable company, if you don't turn those profits into cash through collecting your receivables, you will be out of business.

Once cash and materials come in the door, take steps to protect them. Great procedures keep your honest employees honest. They show that you are watching and checking. There is less temptation when procedures are in place and monitored.

Here is a summary of the procedures to implement. Details are in the stories in this book.

- Send your bank statements home. This is the first line of defense. Make sure the checks are correct and your signature is on all checks. Look at the pictures of the checks. Look at deposits and withdrawals. If something doesn't look right, question it. Once you have looked at the bank statement, bring it to the bookkeeper to balance the checkbook.

- Your bookkeeper should never have check signing authority (unless your bookkeeper is your spouse or owns part of the business).
- Balance the checkbook. Make sure you see all the reconciliations of the bank accounts.
- Enter the expenses stated on your P&L into a spreadsheet. You don't have to do it every month. Do it a few times a year.
- Petty cash must be verified each month. If money is taken from petty cash, receipts must be given for that amount. When the petty cash gets low, the amount of the receipts is replaced with a check cashed at your bank.
- Don't keep thousands of dollars in petty cash. Put all amounts over a few hundred dollars in your bank.
- Even if you have two people handling petty cash, the owner should count it occasionally.
- Give a bookkeeping test to prospective bookkeepers. Email me at rking@ontheribbon.com if you would like a free copy of the bookkeeping test and answers.
- Conduct a background check. This should be done for all prospective employees, not just prospective bookkeepers.
- Do drug testing. Many companies also drug screen prior to hiring. This is critical with businesses where employees drive company trucks or go to customers' homes or businesses.
- Consider direct deposit for your payroll checks. When you use direct deposit, employees get a notice of their gross wages and deductions. They

see that a certain amount was put in their checking account. Employees cannot see the company's checking account and bank routing numbers.

- If direct deposit is not an option, have a separate payroll account where you keep just enough money to fund payroll each payroll period.
- Do not use signature stamps. If you require two signatures on checks, they should be two signatures, not a signature and a signature stamp.
- Review financial statements every month. Analyze your balance sheet and profit and loss statement (take a class or read my book *The Courage to Be Profitable*, which explains how to read financial statements in English rather than accountingese).
- Watch what you sign. If a check looks wrong, question it and ask for backup.
- If you can't log in to your employees' computers, walk with the person to their desk and ask them to print out the report you need while you are watching. This prevents changes before the report is given to you.
- Always make sure that payroll taxes are paid. If you file them electronically, the confirmation numbers should be printed out and put somewhere for safekeeping. If the IRS sends you a letter saying the taxes for a quarter were not paid, you can give them the confirmation number showing that you paid the taxes.

- Always make sure that the tax entry is correct. Sometimes the person entering the information enters the correct amount of tax but specifies the wrong quarter. If this happens, the confirmation number shows that the taxes were paid on time but the time period they apply to was wrong. Correct this immediately.

- Check out the financial condition of a company prior to agreeing to work for that company. Even if a company is known, if that company goes bankrupt, your company may have to repay the bankruptcy court any monies received 90 days prior to the bankruptcy filing. Build and keep a cash reserve in this amount as your company is working on the job.

- Collections are critical to cash flow. If a payment has not been received in the time allotted for payment, the bookkeeper must make a call the next day to find out when a payment can be expected. If you don't get a check, stop work. It's hard but necessary to do this.

- The person opening the mail should not be the person who makes the bank deposits.

- Whenever you are handling cash or checks and you leave your desk, lock up the cash and checks. You never know who will pass by your desk and take the cash or a check.

- Make copies of all the checks and cash. You might need to refer to the copies at a later date.

- Owners or a company manager should be the only ones allowed to enter new vendors into the bookkeeping system. The bookkeeper should be locked out of adding new vendors to your accounting software.

- Print out a vendor list once per quarter. Make sure there are no duplicate names. If you don't know how to do it, watch the bookkeeper as she does it.

- Always require backup for any checks you sign. This can include purchase orders, packing slips showing receipt of materials, and vendor invoiced. Make sure they match!

- Train your employees not to accept postdated checks. The checks should be written and dated the day the work was performed.

- Train your employees to look at the date on the check.

- Lunch breaks are for lunch. Employees should not be eating at the office after they take their hour lunch break. This policy should be clear in your employee handbook.

- Check with the labor laws of your state. Some states require breaks and lunch periods that must be taken by employees. Follow your state regulations.

- All checks, whether from customers or blank company checks, should be kept under lock and key.

- Customer checks should be immediately stamped with "for deposit only" and the account number, and the deposit should be made quickly.

- The financial information you receive at the end of each month should include the reconciliation report showing that your accounting software cash balance matches the bank cash balance.

- Using an outside firm to process your payroll can save time for your company. Interview many and determine which one gives you the most value for your money.

- Whenever using outside payroll firms always check to see that the payroll tax deposits have been made. The payroll company should give you the reports that they have been made. Check these with the Internal Revenue Service and your state and local departments of revenue.

- Make sure your bookkeeper matches revenues and expenses incurred to generate those revenues each month. If your gross margins are not consistent on a monthly basis, find out why.

- Have an inventory policy in place. There should be a procedure for ordering materials, getting materials to the jobsite or production line, and returning materials.

- Inventory should be counted at least once per year. If you find problems, it should be counted more often—monthly if required—until the problems are resolved.

- The person opening the mail should not make the bank deposits. This may not be practical for smaller companies, but it is preferable that owners make bank deposits whenever possible.

- See all of the cash withdrawals from your checking account. It is best to look at your bank balances online every day. You can see everything that is added and withdrawn from your accounts.

- Insist that everyone take at least a week's vacation. This way someone else has to do that person's job. This is when you find discrepancies.

- Get your financial statements on time. It's hard to remember what happened 90 days ago. January's statements should be prepared by February 10 or at the latest February 15.

- Always match aged accounts receivable and accounts payable report balances to the amounts stated on your balance sheet.

- Ask for month-end journal entries when you receive your financial statements. Make sure that they make sense.

- A good purchase order system is necessary. Make sure that purchase orders are filled out completely, including the materials purchased, the person making the order, and the price of the materials.

- The CPA firm who prepares your taxes should do a yearly review. They can also spot things that don't balance or look right. An outside firm looking at the numbers gives you peace of mind.

- Always track cash coming into the business. Make sure that all cash received is deposited in your operations checking account.

- If your employees regularly receive cash payments, there should be a maximum amount they are allowed to have without coming to the office to turn in cash.

- For retail operations, determine the maximum amount of cash that you will keep in the cash registers. Pull amounts over that limit and put them in the safe until a bank deposit can be made.

- Always know when payroll taxes, sales taxes, and other payments are due. Put them on your calendar. Check on the due date to ensure the payments have been prepared or paid. Many of them are now done through direct withdrawals. In these cases, make sure you see the confirmation numbers proving that the payments have been made.

- Determine the cost for doing every project your company works on. Calculate your company's overhead cost per hour (total overhead divided by the number of revenue producing or billable hours) and the net profit per hour (total net profit divided by the number of hours on that project) for each project.

- If you use an outside service to handle calls in the evenings and weekends, that service should give you a list of all calls they received and took messages for during that time period. Give this report to a manager who is responsible for making sure that the company got paid for the work it did, even on weekends.

- Enforce company policies, even when it hurts to lose an employee. It sends a message to the remaining employees that the company is serious about enforcement and is fair to all employees.

- Always track cash payments. For restaurants, have a system for entering food purchases and match the purchases to the payments. It takes some time to do this, especially if you are doing it manually. However, it is critical because it is tempting to take cash.
- If you find a mistake, investigate it immediately. Then watch to see whether the mistake is corrected. You are sending a message that you are watching to all employees.
- If you do need large amounts of cash on hand, don't have the same weekly routine for getting it and storing it. It becomes a great temptation to steal when many people know the routine cash procedure.
- Always make an adding machine tape of your deposit and copy the cash and checks that make up the deposit.
- Calculate the revenue you need to generate to pay for one hour of overtime. Of course, if by paying that one hour of overtime each week you can generate the additional revenues, you should gladly pay it.
- If your office employees are paid on a salary basis, you may still have to pay overtime. Check with the Department of Labor in your state.
- Look at your payroll each week. If your employees are consistently receiving an hour or two of overtime each week, make them justify the additional hours. They might have gotten used to the additional money and are finding a

way to stretch their time to receive that extra income each month.

- If you have company credit cards, whenever an employee uses a credit card for a company purchase, verify that purchase. When the statements come in at the end of the month, verify that all purchases on that statement have receipts for what was purchased. Question things that don't make sense.

- Always issue company mobile phones if your employees take business calls during the day. Then you can see the types of calls received on that mobile phone.

- Always balance your credit card statements against receipts. If receipts are missing, find out why.

- Many companies implement a "no receipt, no payment" policy. It ensures that you get the receipts. Look at them to make sure they are legitimate. Yes, it takes time. However, it is your hard-earned cash that could be paying for employees' personal expenses.

- Always require project or job numbers on any purchase order for materials. This way you can track these numbers and know all materials purchased for that project.

- Review your statements from your vendors. Make sure that material purchases have a purchase order number, a packing slip showing the materials were received, and the price on the purchase order is the price on the invoice before the bill is paid.

- Cameras in offices and warehouses are becoming common and should be considered. It may not be employees stealing, but outsiders coming in to your office or warehouse. If you can see them on a camera, you have a better chance of catching them.

- Count inventory each year so you will have an accurate figure for your balance sheet and your taxes. You can see what the shrinkage, if any, was. If there was shrinkage, take steps to track it carefully.

- Put 1% of your receipts away. Every time you make a bank deposit, take 1% of that deposit and put it in a savings account. If your savings account is at the same bank as your operating account, it is easy to transfer money between the two accounts.

- If you use the money from your savings account, always repay it when extra cash comes in the door. This is the only way to ensure that cash is available when you might need it.

- Whenever payments are received from field employees, the person receiving them must initial the paperwork that the payments were received by that person. This way you can track the money trail if there is a problem.

- Sign all checks, and watch what you sign.

FINAL THOUGHTS

Embezzlers and thieves will hate this book. I revealed many of the ways they steal from you. The second story in the book was something I never dreamed of, and it was the first time in more than 35 years that I had ever seen this type of theft.

The Ugly Truth about Cash helps keep the honest people honest. These are the people who usually think rationally but because of a personal situation think emotionally and do stupid things. When these processes are in place and they know that you are watching, there is less temptation to steal money because they know they will get caught.

Now my warning to the remaining 1%: Revealing your practices in this book will force you to be even more diabolically creative in your theft. I hope you can't figure out another way to steal, but if you do, I will hear about it and write a sequel to this book revealing the new ways you have found to steal.

THANK YOU TO...

This book would never have been written without you, my small business clients, over the past 35 years. I've seen your joys. I've seen the pain when I gently helped you discover that someone was embezzling. Thank you for allowing me to help you grow profitably. As one of you said, I have been responsible for many of the highest highs and lowest lows in your life. I hope there have been many more highs than lows for you.

Brenda Bethea has been my "right arm" for more than 25 years. She has participated in the growth, heard your stories, and been in the trenches with me for this entire journey.

To my parents, who guided my early years and helped shape the woman I have become. Although I didn't always appreciate your actions, you were always there to pick up the pieces when I made mistakes and cheer me on when I was working to achieve a goal.

To my husband, Bob, who during that last conversation we had told me to "Do my thing." This book is a result of our conversation.

And finally to my daughter, Kate, your journey is under way. I hope that you find happiness and success.

Use the stories in this book to keep you from the heartache that many other business owners have faced.

Thank you all. I love and appreciate you.

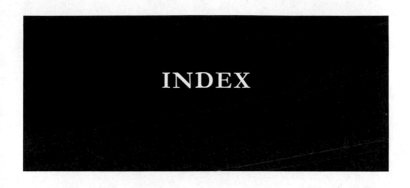

INDEX

T

V

W

ABOUT THE AUTHOR

Profitability master Ruth King is founder and CEO of Profitability Revolution Paradigm. She is also president of Business Ventures Corporation. Ruth has a passion for helping small businesses get and stay profitable.

She is especially proud of one small business owner she helped climb out of a big hole. He started with a negative $400,000 net worth 15 years ago and is still in business today...profitably and with a positive net worth.

After 12 years on the road, doing 200 flights per year, she knew there had to be a better way to reach businesspeople who wanted to build their businesses and train their employees. She began training on the Internet in 1998 and began the first television like broadcasting in 2002. Her channels include www.hvacchannel.tv, 24/7/365 broadcasting on www.profitabilityrevolution.com, and others.

Ruth holds an MBA in finance from Georgia State University and bachelor's and master's degrees in chemical engineering from Tufts University and the University of Pennsylvania, respectively.

She started the Decatur, Georgia, branch of the Small Business Development Center in 1982. She also started the Women's Entrepreneurial Center and taught a yearlong course for women who wanted to start their own businesses. This course was the foundation for one of the classes at the Women's Economic Development Authority in Atlanta, Georgia.

More recently Ruth was the instructor for the Inner City Entrepreneur (ICE) program in conjunction with the Small Business Administration. This 16-week course taught business owners with at least $400,000 in revenues (and many had over $1 million in revenues) how to grow to the next level. A large part of the curriculum was aimed at improving the financial knowledge of the business owners enrolled in the course.

Ruth is passionate about helping adults learn to read, photography, and marathon races (she has run 14, including two Boston Marathons). She helped start an adult literacy organization in 1986 that currently serves more than 1,000 adults per year.

Her number 1 best-selling book, *The Courage to Be Profitable*, explains how to get and stay profitable in less than 30 minutes a month—in English rather than accounting babble. She is also the author of two other award-winning books: *The Ugly Truth about Small Business* and *The Ugly Truth about Managing People*. You can contact Ruth at rking@ontheribbon.com.